TAKE YOUR CHARACTERS TO DINNER

Creating the Illusion of Reality in Fiction

A Creative Writing Course

Laurel A. Yourke

University Press of America,® Inc.
Lanham • New York • Oxford

University Press of America,® Inc.
4501 Forbes Boulevard, Suite 200
Lanham, Maryland 20706

12 Hid's Copse Rd.
Cumnor Hill, Oxford OX2 9JJ

Library of Congress Cataloging-in-Publication Data

Yourke, Laurel A.
Take your characters to dinner : creating the illusion of
reality in fiction : a creative writing course b/ Laurel A. Rourke.
p.   cm.
Includes bibliographical references and index.
1. Fiction—Authorship. 2. Creative writing. I. Title.
PN3355.Y68   2000   808.3—dc21   00-029864 CIP

ISBN 0-7618-1694-1 (pbk: alk. ppr)

3 1559 00171 7584

∞™ The paper used in this publication meets the minimum
requirements of American National Standard for Information
Sciences—Permanence of Paper for Printed Library Materials,
ANSI Z39.48—1984

TABLE OF CONTENTS

ACKNOWLEDGEMENTS

I feel blessed to be surrounded by the talented people who have made enormous contributions to this book: Emily Auerbach for guidance, Carol Beck for support, Maxine Beck for alertness, David Berger for faith, Marshall Cook for insight, Brendan Day for creativity, Christine DeSmet for precision, Kim Fowler for crispness, Mary Magray for thoroughness, Jan Schubert for acumen, Rob Rhode-Szudy for technological artistry, Bob Wilson for expertise, and last but not least, my mother—for so much.

I am grateful to the following authors for their willingness to enrich this book with their work:

Betsy Alberts	"Mary's kids"
Jane Wright Anderson	"The Mirror"
Marv Beatty	"Lefty"
David Berger	"Ted Cody"
Sarah Brooks	"The Sauna"
Ruth Calden	"The Green-Eyed Monster"
Marshall J. Cook	*The Year of the Buffalo* (Excerpt, by permission of the author)
Christine DeSmet	*Spirit Lake* (Excerpt, by permission of the author)
Helen Dyer	"Mrs. Dunbar"
Judith Gaskell	"Meta White"
Lisa Glueck	"Down Haven"
Frank Lusson	"South of Quincey" (Excerpt, by permission of the author)
Melissa Paton	"The Cookie Chairman"
Yenna Phillips	"From Meat and Potatoes to Caviar"
Jan Schubert	"Artwork"
Jan Schubert	"North Woods"
Gail Sterkel	"His Beard"
Deborah Woodworth	*A Deadly Shaker Spring* (Excerpt, by permission of HarperCollins)

PREFACE

Fictional Reality and Feeding Your Characters

*"All fiction for me is a kind of magic and trickery—a confidence trick, trying to make people believe something is true that isn't."
(Angus Wilson in Collins, 50)*

DINING OUT WITH GEORGINA AND HER CHARACTERS

Sprawled across the lilac coverlet on her gigantic bed, Georgina imagines the characters of her novel chatting in her bedroom. She visualizes them tidying up the remnants of a gourmet picnic they just polished off. Winding her fingers through her long red hair, Georgina escorts Henry Petry, her protagonist, away from the other characters. "Want a cashew?" she offers. "They're jumbo."

Henry glares at her. "Won't it be dinner time soon? How 'bout treating us to something Vietnamese and fancy, heavy on the lemongrass."

Georgina frowns. "Not so fast. You've barely finished this meal. Going to break down and ask your dad for advice?"

"No comment till you serve up something with curry."

Before Georgina finishes nodding, her imagination whisks Henry, his dad and mom dragging a few steps behind, into a room of starched tablecloths and lacquered bowls of diced scallions, salted nuts, and dipping sauce. Mrs. Petry lifts her chopsticks, then drops them. "Why would anyone eat this?" Her chopsticks make a little thud. She studies her nails, thinking how a new ring would set them off. Mr. Petry shoots her a look while Henry memorizes the soy sauce label. "In my opinion," Mrs. Petry begins...

Georgina leans back to listen.

Week by week Georgina becomes more experienced with taking her characters to dinner to discover how they sound and who they are. "Every time this family argues, mom evaluates her manicure." Georgina makes a mental note. "Henry reads whatever he can find. Useful details." Georgina plants a moist kiss on the orange tabby snoozing beside her. She can almost picture her first chapter.

Character and plot no longer terrorize her. Now they just make her a little anxious. Sometimes she stops in the middle of a draft to whine, "Nothing's happening! They sit around babbling." Once she tried to salvage a floundering section by chasing a litter of kittens across her pages. But felines don't enrich plot in fiction about the Galapagos Islands. So these days Georgina feeds her characters at restaurant after restaurant until she knows them inside and out. She substitutes deep understanding for contrived devices.

Every writer needs far more background material, especially about the characters, than actually materializes in the fiction. Intimate knowledge of every character offers security, an investment that resembles purchasing extra cans of tomato paste. That way, no matter how often you feel like spaghetti, reserves line the back of your cabinet—and ideas for characterization and plot wait their turn at the back of your mind.

Few writers interview every character. Yet you must know your main characters so intimately that they become more lifelike than the people that you encounter at the office or supermarket. Unless characters are real to you they never come to life for your readers. As a fiction writer, your goal is to—*abracadabra!*—manufacture rabbits, or at least their illusion, out of thin air. Fiction works its magic by creating a version of reality that ironically seems more realistic than reality. Without intimate knowledge of your characters and their world, you can't originate that impression.

ISOLATING THE HIGHER TRUTHS OF FICTION

The source of a believable fictional world is vital characters. Those characters help readers infer any truths that fiction possesses. Verisimilitude is a hefty word that captures a hefty concept: art, in this case fiction, portrays a simulation—a representation of reality and truth. Fiction offers a better-crafted, more credible, faster moving version of reality. And why not? Life often seems humdrum or improbable. Too much bad (or good!) luck happens at once. Long-lost friends encounter each other in airports thousands of miles from where either one lives, and problems resolve themselves (or fail to) without rhyme or reason. People accept such coincidences as true because they happened. In fiction, though, writers must convince readers that events seem believable and feel true.

Sometimes people find life not only improbable, but, too often, unfair—even immoral. Good Samaritans die in poverty, while creeps flaunt winning lottery tickets. Another truth of fiction involves morality: within reason, characters get what they deserve. This poetic justice conveys the impression of order, which Aristotle viewed as one of the underpinnings of beauty. Readers want fiction to organize the pandemonium of life, to suggest the pattern residing beneath the disorder. That pattern suggests an ultimate truth.

Checklist: The Higher Truths of Fiction

✓ Credibility
✓ Probability
✓ Order

✓ Morality
✓ Beauty
✓ Intrigue

WEDDING PERSPIRATION AND MAGIC

As a writer you can integrate seemingly conflicting levels of truth by combining surges of inspiration with deliberate crafting. You're probably familiar with the arguments over whether writing can be taught. That dispute will persist forever because both sides are right. All writers instinctively accomplish certain tasks without conscious planning, and all writers benefit from deeper understanding and attention to craft. Why discount one when both diligence and spontaneity contribute?

From time to time, most writers compose pages effortlessly. Doesn't this seem magical? Yet that *magic* resides neither in black hats nor white rabbits but in knowing your characters well enough to make them real: first to you, then to your readers. Familiarity with the characters helps you conjure all those complex levels of truth. Hmm. Characterization alone doesn't necessarily reveal truth or even produce good fiction. Neither does the magical component often labeled *talent*. Writers usually need to understand fiction's elements and then incorporate these through revision.

INTRODUCTION

The Reality of Writing Fiction

> *"I have no shrewd advice to offer developing writers about this business of snatching time and space to work. I do not have anything profound to offer mother-writers or worker-writers except to say that it will cost you something. Anything of value is going to cost you something." (Toni Cade Bambara in Shaughnessy, 10)*

EXAMINING THE STRUCTURE OF THIS BOOK

This text isolates the fundamentals that help fiction writers work their magic. Needless to say, separating integrated elements seems artificial. Every aspect of fiction impacts every other, the way the amount of sugar you add to bread dough affects how much yeast you need. To create a perfect loaf, you must balance ingredients baked for the correct amount of time and enhanced with the right polishing glaze. At some point, then, you must consider the entire recipe—not just the yeast.

Yet when honing skills either in your kitchen or fiction, investigating one component at a time can help. So writing teachers often approach the craft of fiction via arbitrary divisions like character, plot, and setting. The first time Georgina thought about more than one fictional element at once, anxiety glued her to her ancient television set for an entire weekend. To escape her experience, consider skimming this entire book before contemplating how to put everything together.

GENERATING A COMMITMENT

Reading about writing is the easy part.

"Muffin," Georgina informs one of her two cats, "I hate those silly writing books promising, *Can You Breathe? Then You Can Write!* Neither finches, ferrets, nor flying lizards create, although all of them exhale. Few folks produce gorgeous fiction without revision after revision. Truthfully, hunting for food could prove easier than making a living at writing."

Muffin's eyes open at the word "food," then close when he realizes that, as usual, Georgina's babbling doesn't concern him. She shakes the cat gently to get his attention. "Want to hear how I keep going when it feels scary and hard?"

Georgina's Ten Top Writing Tips

✓ Write nearly every day, even if only for ten minutes. (Half an hour is better.) No cheating.

✓ Talk to your characters often. Let people think you're slightly crazy. It's okay.

✓ Focus on your characters—not the clever or profound point you want to prove.

✓ Keep your characters on firm ground rather than thin air (unless they're spirits).

✓ Make something happen. Make readers believe that what happened matters to them.

✓ Revise constantly. Learn to love it.

✓ Discard words and ideas. Toss them to the wind. Learn to love that, too.

✓ Pay attention to ideas that interrupt when you're not writing. Such moments spawn the brightest material.

✓ Have fun writing. If you're not, your readers probably won't either.

✓ Believe in yourself. (You needn't admit this to anyone.)

Deep breathing won't get you a bestseller. But there's good news. Everyone—without exception—can learn to write better.

PUSHING OFF

How does that process begin? Where do you get an idea, integrate the elements of fiction, and then bake up something bubbling over with flavor and aroma? This book examines the fundamentals of fiction within short stories and novels—two distinct fictional forms. The short story represents a light lunch, not a full-course meal. To let readers digest a small portion without feeling overfed, the short story should focus on only a few incidents. Short fiction can rarely manage a huge family or an entire neighborhood, nor resolve all the world's problems in fewer than ten pages.

Short or long, all fiction springs to life from a character, plot, or image. This is only the first step. As Bonnie Friedman discovered,

> Writing school turned out to be all about grammar, the grammar of fiction, the syntax and inflection of rhetorical choices. Strategy was talked about a lot here, as if a story consisted of troops on various maneuvers. How did you deploy your forces? How did you manage your subject's inherent strengths, and compensate for its weaknesses? (Friedman, 50-51)

"Grammar of fiction"? Grammar intimidates many people, and few writers diagram their sentences. Yet everyday use of language lets most people internalize a certain amount of grammar. Similarly, the more people read, the more instinctive the basic "grammar of fiction" becomes. Reading the kind of fiction one wants to write accelerates the process. Dissecting that fiction performs the same function as diagramming sentences—but most people enjoy reading more.

WRITING AND READING

Exhaustive and intensive reading hones writing skill. According to Adrienne Rich, "You must write, and read, as if your life depended on it. That is not generally taught in school." (Rich, 32) To ripen your writing skill, ripen your reading skill. Reading opens mind and imagination both to information and the universal genealogy of all writers, a family tree that welcomes the newest participants into the stream of history and art.

But if you incorporate everything you know, you'll sink your fiction beneath that weight. Invent more about your characters than you reveal, and your readers benefit. Similarly, your grasp (though not necessarily inclusion!) of history, art, science, and anything else infuses your fiction with greater power. Writing seems richest when you exploit both the linear and intuitive sides of the brain (left and right respectively).

Strategic reading offers information and pleasure along with excursions into the "grammar of fiction." Read like a writer instead of a complacent reader and you learn to write for readers. You differentiate lovely from lumbering sentences and tantalizing characterization from trite portrayal. You discern craft. Such reading refines your thinking about which writing techniques soar—and which thud. Georgina no longer reads without noticing metaphor, point of view, credibility, syntax, and the rest. She's grumpy that her reading feels a little less fun yet impressed that her writing becomes more so.

Planning what to write and read speeds acquisition of skill. Why not complete an effective short story or two before undertaking a novel? The techniques secured in perfecting shorter works facilitate tackling more challenging tasks later. But don't write short stories until you read some—and not just the classics you studied in school. The anthologies listed in the bibliography provide contemporary examples.

KEEPING A JOURNAL

Read and write. Even on days when Georgina must cope with the stress of an indoor cat escaping outdoors, she still makes herself write. Frequent reading and writing maintain a mental space where ideas and words flow easily, just as muscles benefit from daily or weekly rather than monthly exercise.

Keep a journal, and ideas can percolate there until they reach peak flavor. An August inspiration can bubble away for months. By January, though, perhaps you've brewed it to full strength. Journals nourish the writing habit, which, like every habit, needs monitoring. Humorist James Thurber once observed, "I never quite know when I'm not writing. Sometimes my wife comes up to me at a party and says, 'Dammit, Thurber, stop writing.' She usually catches me in the middle of a paragraph." (Winokur, 323) You needn't write mentally every waking moment, and, if you write exclusively in your journal, you won't produce any fiction. Separate the process from the goal.

FINDING SUBJECT MATTER

If your goal is writing fiction, must you sky dive or safari through Africa to unearth material? Intriguing options won't automatically initiate fiction. Its basis is less participation and interaction than observation and, eventually, interpretation. Perception and imagination signify more than actual experience. An ingenious treatment can produce a compelling work about a daydreaming boy who watches ants capture cake crumbs, while a novel describing an exploding volcano can bore everyone. Good writers can intoxicate without Morocco, murder, or morphine addiction.

DEVELOPING PATIENCE AND PERSISTENCE

Learning to intrigue readers demands unique skill, and few people master new skills quickly or easily. Yes, some of us feel comfortable the first time we get behind the wheel of a car. Most people, however, must overcome certain fears and practice difficult maneuvers. Despite this, inexperienced writers frequently grow impatient during the training period. Frustrated, they lower their expectations and ignore their instincts about listening and viewing. On the road, too, some drivers assign blame. They think or even vocalize, "What's taking you so long?" or "Why don't you get it, you jerk?" Either instance can produce disaster. Good drivers watch where they're going, think about the other guy, never fall asleep at the wheel, and dodge dangerous shortcuts.

Good writers do the same.

> Saul Bellow said a researcher once paid him ten thousand dollars to come take some psychological tests in Berkeley—they had Capote there, too—and what they ended up with was the feeling that writers had more willpower. Willpower is a nice nineteenth-century term. And if that's all, it doesn't tell you anything, except maybe that discipline helps. (Delbanco in Neubauer, 120)

It does. Like most skills, good writing demands it. Reading, practice, and persistence can produce the euphoria of writing that exceeds your own expectations. Get to it. Keep at it.

Checklist: Getting Underway

- ✓ Read constantly.
- ✓ Keep a journal.
- ✓ Exercise discipline.
- ✓ Employ patience.
- ✓ Preserve perspective.
- ✓ Sustain your sense of humor.

CHAPTER 1: Credibility

Manufacturing Reality

One must always keep in mind how "if this, then that" must happen. Every detail must mean more than itself. The smallest error in plausibility threatens the credibility of the whole. (Paul Horgan, 42)

HELPING READERS BELIEVE

Georgina's character, Henry, glowers at her, swallowing his distaste over the thin veil of cat fur draping everything. He forces his attention away from the fur and back to his point. "Who does my Mom think she is? She can't talk to me like that. I won't..."

"Henry, Henry, Henry. I'm not the one patronizing you." Georgina smiles tenderly. "Naturally you're determined to confront her. I want you to. At this point, though, it wouldn't seem believable. You haven't shown that kind of courage."

"Says who!"

"Says any novel reader. Henry, being fictitious doesn't give you permission to do whatever you like. Quite the opposite, in fact. Readers quit reading unless characters seem..."

Henry straightens to his full five feet six inches. "I can face my mom. I can tell Ashley how I feel about her. I can ..."

"That's the stuff, Henry. Prove you've got it in you, and I promise to make my readers believe it's so." She looks down at her feet. "Or at least try. But, remember," she shakes her finger at him, "you don't get to be brazen out of thin air."

Credibility pumps the heart of fiction. Georgina knows enough about fiction to insist that her readers find Henry believable. This helps readers cheerfully expand the customary boundaries of reality by suspending their disbelief.

Suspension of disbelief involves an unwritten contract between writer and reader about what constitutes reality. If the writer produces a plausible and consistent environment, then the reader temporarily abandons expectations about normalcy. If the fictional realm seems inviting, within its borders readers accept impossible, or at least improbable, settings, characters, and events. A hulking brute tries to teach his creator how to be human (Mary Shelley's *Frankenstein*); beasts run agribusiness (George Orwell's *Animal Farm*); a friendship revives in another incarnation a century later (Amy Tan's *The Hundred Secret Senses*), or a boy learns wizardry (J.K. Rowling's *Harry Potter and the Sorcerer's Stone*). Readers accept such domains on faith.

CONSTRUCTING NEW WORLDS

Fiction introduces readers to unexplored terrain, although that can be as close as the house next door. Writer helps reader redefine reality within what John Gardner calls "a fictional dream." In his now out-of-print text, *The Art of Fiction*, Gardner contends that "fiction does its work by creating a dream in the reader's mind." (Gardner, 31) Fiction writers fashion a dream world at least as concrete, vivid, and completely credible as those inhabited nightly while we sleep.

In fact, the fiction writer manufactures not just a dream state but a new world—a fictional one—that readers believe they enter. This applies to fiction developed from imagination, reality, or a combination of these. "The fact that a story is true of course does not relieve the novelist [or short story writer] of the responsibility of making the characters and events convincing." (Gardner, 23) Strict adherence to truth can undermine the credibility of your fictional world. Fiction depends first on credibility, then characterization, then everything else.

REVISITING CINDERELLA

Is the fictional world of Cinderella credible? Readers meet jealous stepsisters and their unjust mother mistreating a lovely maiden—no problem there. Involved in this fictional world, the audience accepts that the fairy godmother can render the scullery maid Queen for a Day, complete with resplendent coach and crystal slippers. The transformed Cinderella bewitches the lonely Prince. But midnight terminates all magic. Dawn finds the lovesick Prince scouring his kingdom for an adult woman with a size-four shoe. When the shoe fits, Cinderella gets to wear it forever. Everyone applauds the blissful ending.

Now if the original fairytale manufacturers hadn't fashioned a fictional world, would even the tiniest tots swallow this chain of improbabilities? Yet many adults not only believe but also cherish this enchanted realm where mice become horses, rags change to ermine, and tiny feet guarantee happiness.

Within this fictional world, readers identify with Cinderella and her Prince, experiencing irritation with those mistreating the future princess. But anachronism or inconsistency can shift sympathy, even hurl readers from the fictional realm. What if Cinderella finishes scouring the hearth and begins reconfiguring the household computer? How do wordiness, repetition, or run-on sentences affect absorption in a fictional world? What if information about fairy godmothers in various countries, or data on mouse mating cycles yanks readers back to reality?

The fictional world collapses when writers insert a clashing or distracting circumstance, such as a fairytale transpiring on an alien planet where breath can shatter glass. Readers deserve—and expect—internal consistency within the borders of fairytale, planet Pluto, or mountain village.

PINNING DOWN THE IDEA

What brings a fictional world to life? Some writers get comfortable, maybe reread some journal pages or mentally review an idea, and then...nothing happens. What if a helpless writer such as Georgina stares interminably (and perhaps a little sullenly) at an empty pad or a blank computer monitor? Memory, observation, and imagination can generate fascinating detail. Focus transforms that into the beginnings of fiction.

The Situation

Perhaps a vague impression glimmers near your consciousness, floating just beyond reach. In order to put that possibility to work, remember what fiction readers seek. Fiction involves believable characters facing escalating conflict. With that in mind, evaluate these starting points.

Two brothers try to keep their farm going. But they have a lot of struggles.

She lived alone and didn't like it. Would things ever change?

> This was their first date. She felt somewhat uncomfortable. Hopefully, things would go okay.

Fiction requires a concrete conflict, yet the ideas above sound vague and lifeless. Contrast those examples with the following:

> Sarabeth couldn't see a dog without wanting to bring it home so they could become allies.

> Snow fell so thickly that Tom wondered if he'd recognize his exit—if he got that far alive.

> The blood kept dripping, dripping with the regularity of the metronome that loomed in the background of all Leora's piano lessons.

Narrow your focus, and every subject can germinate fiction.

The Overblown and the Overused

A fresh infusion stimulates material. Fiction that doesn't intrigue its author will never intrigue anyone else. Certain situations seem neither broad nor implausible but tried and true as the girl-scout pledge, predictable as flies on honey, or familiar as your own hand. Decades ago, Eudora Welty observed that "Whatever our theme in writing, it is old and tried. Whatever our place, it has been visited by the stranger, it will never be new again. It is only the vision that can be new; but that is enough." (Charlton, 31)

Readers like surprise. Use the inventive to revitalize the conventional. Boy loses beloved dog; boy finds beloved dog. Why not vary this? The boy's beloved dog escapes because although he regrets leaving his pal, Rover must complete his secret mission. Or the first-year teacher seeks someone to save. This student, though, isn't interested in college and wants to work the impoverished family farm.

Refurbish cliché by changing some aspect of the circumstances. Everyone knows about the criminal breaking into a convenience store and terrorizing the isolated night worker. What happens if the apprehensive criminal narrates the tale? What if you transform the stereotypical criminal into a retired musician? Make the customary startling by shifting either character perspective or reader expectation:

Franklin pulled the cap low over his eyes and sped to the liquor store. Ten minutes till midnight. Good. He still had a little time. Watching the storefront while waiting for a bulky figure to emerge, he inhaled with quick gasps.

Readers foresee yet another lifeless version of a ghetto youth worried about being late to his own robbery. Why not add a twist?

Too hot for a cap, the youth decided—no matter how good it looked. Franklin grinned, so excited he could hardly breathe. By the time his favorite uncle got off work around midnight, Franklin would be ready with a bottle of champagne to celebrate his mentor's sixty-fifth birthday.

This version begins developing character and delivering the unexpected.

Vitality

A new perspective can energize the most exhausted subjects. Change the slant; probe beneath the surface; intertwine plot with subplot, or flesh out a few examples rather than introducing familiar or distracting characters, images, and episodes. Deepen the canyon of your fiction. Don't construct an ever-widening, ever-flat plain. Broad, shallow scope impedes originality.

Why not sharpen your focus right at the start? You can add complexity at any point, but it's often easier to develop a situation you restricted before proceeding far. Imagine positioning a camera this way and that until the dominant image emerges in the exact center of an imaginary camera frame. You needn't locate anything new within that scope—only something new to say about whatever you center there.

Georgina wasn't always concerned with credibility, focus, and originality. "I'm just writing for myself," she explained to Cinnamon, who was a tiny kitty back then. Now that Cinnamon weighs fourteen pounds and Georgina hopes to publish someday, she envisions an audience more critical than her two felines. After all, the cats just lick themselves, unconcerned whether Georgina revises—or doesn't. Georgina looks up from her first chapter, which she's been reading aloud to decide how it sounds. "Hey! Wake up! You didn't hear a word, did you?"

Cinnamon sleeps on.

"This is why I need a larger audience. You guys wouldn't trade a lick of milk for what my fiction says or how it says it. This isn't ready yet. But someday I'd like to share with someone who cares."

TRANSPORTING YOUR AUDIENCE

Identify your audience. Perhaps it sounds trivial to mention that audience affects many writing decisions. Do you write only for self, friends, family, and pets, or for those who don't know you?

Public Writing versus Journal Writing

A public audience demands different requirements. Within a journal's pages or when sharing with loved ones, you can disregard wordiness, repetition, even standard grammar. Neither clarity nor magnetism matter, since readers already regard both you and your prose with sympathetic interest. Alas, this won't work with a public audience. You must convince them that they care about what you have to say.

Writer Jane Wright Anderson offers this distinction between public and private writing:

> Writing for yourself is like combing and parting your hair without a mirror. If you don't get the part in your hair straight you probably won't know, and you might not even care. When you write for others, your audience becomes your mirror. Their perceptions of your work may surprise you, but you must consider their opinion about whether your part is straight or not.

If you send your writing outside, readers expect a fictional world that makes sense and matters. Readers want characters to resemble real people engaged in conflicts that generate empathy. As a writer, you must decide whether you care what others think of your hair—and your fiction.

Fundamental Ground Rules

If you accept responsibility for your readers and how your writing affects them, you pledge allegiance to credibility, coherence, and characterization. The following guidelines help maintain that commitment. Like most generalizations, these principles don't always pertain. Exceptions exist. Yet these standards eliminate everything that separates your characters from your readers.

1. Maintain Invisibility.

George Orwell urged writers to be invisible as a windowpane. Never block the reader's view of the characters and their experiences. Show; don't tell. This principle seemingly clashes with another familiar command: state the main idea, illustrate it, and reiterate the thesis in your conclusion. This formula for the essay sometimes motivates fiction writers to "tell." Yet even in our information-oriented age, readers turn to fiction more for characterization than information. For centuries, people have cherished fiction for its storytelling capacity. The elements of story—characters and their fate—often include fact and impart theme. But facts and themes remain secondary. Fiction derives its potential force from readers' vicarious participation in experience. Otherwise, why not read nonfiction?

Readers dislike instruction (which feels like command). Writers sometimes hope to influence readers by telling. Yet showing mounts a stronger case. Unless the tone is satirical, the typical reader scorns interruptions resembling, "And now, dear reader, comes the crucial moment ..." Readers want to identify that crucial moment themselves while watching the characters grow, pay for their mistakes, or escape their just desserts. Naturally, conveying theme through character behavior requires greater effort—and trust—from the writer. Writers must rely on both characters and readers: the former to impart ideas, the latter to receive them.

As writers move toward showing theme rather than telling it, confusion can arise over telling what a writer can show versus providing essential exposition.

Exposition: Communicating the background material to clarify character relationship, situation, and conflict.

> "Nothing quite like spring in New York," she whispered to no one in particular, thinking how she'd spent too many of her thirty-two springs in places she liked considerably less.

In this example of exposition, readers discover the age of the protagonist, the setting of the fiction, and something about the protagonist's character. The writer sets up the fictional world.

Telling: Summarizing judgments most readers prefer to
                    conclude on their own.

> She had a nasty habit of muttering out loud, making public what
> should remain private. People disliked her for it, although no one had
> the courage to say so.

The writer tells readers how to react to the character and her "nasty
habit" while explaining that others "disliked her."

Showing: Revealing or illustrating details about character and
                    conflict, thus letting readers draw their own
                    conclusions.

> Unaware that others noticed her grumbling about traffic, smog, and
> strangers, she sauntered down Fifth Avenue.

The writer reveals the protagonist's behavior without judgment or
comment. Readers can draw their own conclusions.

> "Henry," Georgina calls, "I need your help."
> "What now?"
> "Do you feel most people learn from mistakes made in their first
> relationship and go on to ..."
> "I haven't the slightest idea."
> "Thanks for nothing. I'm stuck, and you're no help." Georgina
> turns on the light to view her protagonist better. "Henry, did you know
> your mom's best friend was briefly married at nineteen?"
> "Sandy Barnard? Really?"
> "Your piano teacher, too, you told me."
> "But Mrs. Barnard's always been ..."
> Georgina looks from the evening's first star back to Henry. "Any
> opinion yet?"
> "I'll let you know."
> "Good, then you can let my readers know, too."

Georgina can use Henry to show her own feelings about second
chances. Like many writers, Georgina experiences the strongest
temptation to tell either when introducing a new scene or character or
approaching the conclusion—her final opportunity to share her
invaluable insights on marriage, the greenhouse effect, and the national

debt. Georgina constantly reminds herself to trust Henry's ability to convey her ideas.

2. Startle.

Readers enjoy a new idea, a new slant. Transform the ordinary to the new. A character learning that opposites never attract can surprise readers. Lectures about judging books by their covers no longer can.

3. Foster credibility.

Innovation won't matter unless readers suspend disbelief, or disregard the customary boundaries of reality while visiting a fictional world. You can encourage this leap of faith by developing at least one detail that convinces readers. That can be the freckles on the android's face, the off-color jokes of the horse serving drinks at the bar, or the nap habits of the toddler advising the world's most distinguished physicists.

Details should connect your fictional world with the real one. Deliberate interweaving of fact with fantasy can invent whole new vistas. Unless the scene occurs on another planet, though, keep setting consistent with the world here on earth. In science fiction, of course, you can manufacture a fifth season, a second moon—whatever you like. Even then, every detail must make the fictional world seem more believable. As Mark Twain asked, "Why shouldn't truth be *stranger* than fiction? Fiction, after all, has to make sense." (Winokur, 124)

4. Move outside self.

Sensibly or otherwise, writers often write about themselves. Yet readers sometimes remain unresponsive until writers render their subjective experience universal. Good writing personalizes the worlds of those from other eras, nations, and even planets. Readers enter those worlds most comfortably when the characters, scenes, and themes become universal. How does this happen? One individual's experience represents the experiences of a much larger group of individuals. Readers feel curiosity over how seemingly different people are alike— not how seemingly different people are different! Fiction must reveal the broad significance of a singular experience. Otherwise, only readers interested either in that author or those conditions or characters can participate. Such connections occur, of course, but a perspective relevant to a general audience involves more readers.

5. Exploit perspective.

When effective, point of view, or the narrator's first-, second-, or third-person recounting of events, disappears within the storyline. Readers who observe the point of view have left the fictional world. But point of view should escape only the reader's attention, because perspective determines reactions to protagonists and their troubles. Writers must choose point of view consciously, not just conveniently.

Point of view can intensify or hinder emotional impact. Charles Dickens conveys *Great Expectations* through the eyes of an adult ruminating on his childhood. This cautionary tale has remained relevant for nearly a century and a half because readers relate to one individual gradually distinguishing wrong from right, villain from hero, and gentleman from slob. A different narrator would shape a different story. What if Pip communicated events as child rather than adult? Writers can learn much from noticing point of view in everything they read. Sometimes, though, experimentation alone reveals which point of view offers the most advantages, or even the fewest disadvantages, for each narrative.

6. Focus narrowly.

Years ago, Georgina wrote everything in first person point of view, using the broadest possible scope. The number of pages she could crank out in a single hour amazed her! Speed now impresses her less. She seeks comfort for her readers—not herself. Techniques friendly to writers aren't always friendly to readers. When fiction encompasses a vast panorama, the writer must guide the reader's eye. For example, Mark Twain's *Huckleberry Finn* introduces the many people Huck encounters over many miles of Mississippi River. Yet the book remains one boy's story, emphasizing his personal journey toward distinguishing morality from hypocrisy.

7. Milk metaphor.

Lack of focus also diminishes the impact of figurative language. When you use non-literal comparisons, develop a single relationship. Eliminate the many other possibilities, however intriguing. Related images reinforce mood or pattern. You distract readers if the sun is first a golden eye, then a giant yellow daisy, next an egg yolk, and finally a gleaming coin hurling arrows of heat at the frail humans below. Such mixing generates outright confusion when readers try to visualize coins in terms of eyelashes, flowers, food, and weapons.

Writers often pile up conflicting examples because they lack confidence in the central metaphor. If neither yolk nor coin describes the sun, the writer should find a stronger example. Then a few variations suffice. Tedious references frustrate as much as clashing comparisons. Development without repetition, however, can generate enormous power. Consider the lingering impact of that white whale thrashing between angry sun and violent sea in Herman Melville's *Moby Dick.*

8. Select detail judiciously.

Moby Dick remains one of the great American novels, yet a good editor would have tightened it. Material on Cetaceans drowns Melville's readers. All that information distracts from character and conflict. Inexperienced writers sometimes feel that if some detail is good, then, logically, more detail is better. Random details, however, lead readers astray. Again, like adroit photographers, writers should choose details that help readers focus and follow the storyline. Selection of detail differs from brevity, because the issue isn't necessarily omitting details but providing the right ones to set the scene, clarify patterns, generate mood, or reinforce theme.

9. Link ideas.

Apt details also help readers glide from scene to scene or paragraph to paragraph. Transitions let readers conceptualize how each new development relates to the whole. Every time readers pause to supply an implicit connection they depart from the fictional world. Seamless links permit uninterrupted progress through that realm. In a coherent fictional world, those connections emerge easily. If a writer must battle to hitch one scene to the next, other structural weaknesses exist. The writer might feel grateful that searching for a transition revealed a deeper problem.

10. Clarify.

Writing that lacks transitions or coherence often lacks readability as well. Some consider clarity optional. After all, people still read the novels of James Joyce, the Quartets of T.S. Eliot, and the Cantos of

Ezra Pound. How many people? Outside academia, more people mention these works than appreciate them. Besides, *difficult* and *unclear* aren't synonymous.

Long ago, someone initiated a rumor that English teachers treasure indigenously and idiosyncratically recondite or ostentatiously and ludicrously abstruse verbiage. (Note the effect!) This rumor has spawned incorrect constructions like *inabstrusiveness*. Vague or ambiguous writing doesn't signal profound thinking. Making the complex accessible imparts a greater gift.

11. Understate.

You provide another gift by letting your readers walk your fictional world in place of hearing about it (showing versus telling). When you tell your readers how to react, they can neither participate directly nor draw their own conclusions about a reality less often black or white than shades of gray. Naturally, readers resent being misled, manipulated, or blocked from interaction with the characters. Let your characters' actions speak louder than your words.

12. Delete ruthlessly.

Characters can't captivate if describing them takes forever. Reiterating, explaining, modifying, and providing five examples where one would suffice waste reader time. Writers occasionally cite patriarchs like Charles Dickens who got paid by the word and consequently used as many as possible. In contemporary fiction, though, such examples remain exceptional. The writer can't disappear behind the scenes while burying readers in excess. Discarding the first half of the first page sometimes helps, because opening passages often provide exposition but omit conflict. After speeding up the opening, remove superfluous diction, description, characters, and scenes throughout. Lean is in, excess out.

Accountability to readers underlies every suggestion above.

Checklist: Writing Fundamentals

- ✓ Maintain invisibility.
- ✓ Startle.
- ✓ Foster credibility.
- ✓ Move outside yourself.
- ✓ Exploit perspective.
- ✓ Focus narrowly.
- ✓ Milk metaphor.
- ✓ Select detail judiciously.
- ✓ Link ideas.
- ✓ Clarify.
- ✓ Understate.
- ✓ Delete ruthlessly.

GETTING UNDERWAY

You've considered subject matter, credibility, and audience. The next step is lifting a pen or planting yourself behind a keyboard. Make a start, then keep going.

Checklist: Conquering Block

- ✓ Visualize your way into the clear.

Picture your problem, obstacle, pattern, or rut as having a physical shape, i.e., a boulder blocking an enticing path into the woods, a dangerously deep rut in your driveway, a frozen computer screen. Visualize yourself removing the obstacle. Take your time, but really struggle. Would you seek help or lick this on your own? Get the job done. Then savor the world you want to explore. Nothing gets in your way. It's a free path, and you earned it.

- ✓ Give yourself permission to try.

Who said you should be perfect? That restriction makes it hard to experiment, change, or grow. Could it be okay, just once, to seem second-rate or even to fail? Such permission can generate innovative, possibly superior material. If you feel courageous, in the privacy of your own home, without anyone watching, fail on purpose—just to watch yourself emerge breathing, even smiling!

✓ Shake things up.

> Rearrange. If you write first thing in the morning, try it late at night. If you never reread what you wrote last week, do so. If you detest knowing the last line before you reach the end, invent possible conclusions. All sorts of things can happen—many of them good.

✓ Consider what your writing means to you—and what it doesn't.

> Close your eyes and hear the sounds (not the voices!) of the setting for your fiction.

✓ Identify your own unwritten laws and rules. Question their validity.

✓ Don't censor a single idea or word of your first draft.

✓ Picture yourself through the eyes of the reader who most values your work.

✓ Promise yourself that you can do anything. Listen.

✓ Imagine declining a publication offer. Refuse vehemently.

STRETCHING EXERCISES

My students often find that exercises spark some of their best ideas for fiction, possibly because assignments can liberate writers from their own expectations. After all, it's an exercise, not a serious piece of writing. Then again, maybe not. The exercises that end each chapter can provide structure, set goals, develop skills, and generate ideas.

1. Compose a sample synopsis.

   Jot down an idea for a short story or novel you'd write if you had all the writing skill and all the time in the world.

2. Deconstruct something traditional.

   Create something fresh from something familiar, such as Sleeping Beauty, Bambi, Casey at the Bat. Revamp the opening, the ending, the conflict, or the point of view. For example, how would the Big Bad Wolf narrate Little Red Riding Hood's story? What if the Prince fell madly in love with Cinderella's older sister? Unleash your imagination.

3. Generate two versions geared to distinct audiences.

   Take a broad subject, such as fans waiting to enter a stadium, a blackout crippling a city, a deep-sea fishing expedition. Pitch each version to a different group.

LOOKING BACK, THEN AHEAD

"I can't write another word. Wonder what's on ..." Georgina rehearses her rationalizations about eyestrain and exhaustion. In the end, though, she takes a break from her own novel not with TV but a recent bestseller. Reading helps her study fictional worlds covering everything from the Himalayas to the Golden Retriever psyche. She notices which factors affect her residence in a fictional world.

Occasionally, Georgina fumes over interminably reading like a writer, analyzing plot structure and literary devices right along with who done it. "Sometimes I'm too busy dissecting to follow the plot! Who needs this?" Yet casual reading doesn't feed writing. Besides, well-drawn fictional characters stick to your ribs—dinner instead of a series of desserts.

Like Georgina, you can learn much from observing other writers' characters. Which ones convince you? Which technicalities make characterization fail? Believable characters—not theme, setting, description, or even plot—drive mainstream fiction. So your characters must accompany you not just in your fiction but your life.

What shapes a character? Is it attractive appearance or a strong sense of integrity? *Good* characters are less lovely or honest than memorable. This doesn't necessitate wild lifestyles or nasty private habits. Yet consider the connotation of the word *character*. "He's such a character," they say. This suggests someone somehow remarkable. Sometimes, though, characters become remarkable because the writer peels off all the surface layers. Willie Loman, for example, in Arthur Miller's play *Death of a Salesman*, is an ordinary man who becomes extraordinary because the audience penetrates his consciousness.

Georgina shares breakfast, dinner, and lunch with both regular and bizarre folks. She's after particular information. What makes an ordinary character extraordinary?

CHAPTER 2: Characterization

As Many Dimensions as Reality

A writer's knowledge of himself, realistic and unromantic, is like a store of energy on which he must draw for a lifetime; one volt of it properly directed will bring a character alive. (Graham Greene in Shaughnessy, 114)

OFFERING UNIVERSAL CHARACTER AND PLOT

"Henry, if you could have any job in the whole world, what would you do?"

"I like my job. For part time, it's good enough."

"I know." Georgina longs for a good luck charm to counteract her inaccessible character. "I didn't ask about the job you have."

"Who needs the torture of job interviews?"

Georgina twirls a long strand of hair around her fingers. My God, is that a gray one? "Henry, pay attention. I don't have all the time in the world here, you know."

"Who does? That's why I'm not job hunting."

Georgina grabs the questionable hair, snaps it off, smiles, and leans back against an orchid pillow sham. "You like such exotic food, Henry. Bet you'd love to travel around sampling it."

"Who wouldn't?"

"As part of your job, I mean."

Henry stares out his window. Slowly, his expression changes. "Want to hear a secret?"

"Please. I love secrets."

"Once I fantasized photographing a temple in every country. I'd start in the Mediterranean, travel north, and then…"

"Sounds so spiritual. That surprises me." She takes in his wistful expression. "Guess you want that pretty badly."

"Well, less badly than I want to date Ashley."

Will Henry win his Ashley? Will Georgina make Henry captivating enough that his happiness matters to her readers? Will Georgina find a lucky charm to help her manage Henry?

Readers become and stay involved when fiction offers intriguing characters who covet something enough to stimulate action. Static characters interest no one. The tension between what characters have versus what they want or need reveals personality while propelling plot. The intersection of character with plot originates fiction: someone readers identify with craves something and captures it—or tries. However, many writers ignore plot while getting extremely close and personal with at least some of their characters. Georgina enjoys comparing and contrasting her characters' behavior and beliefs with her own.

"Ashley," she muses, sniffing the simmering tomato sauce, "thinks perfume should smell fresh as soap, while I love musk. Guys who drench themselves in expensive after-shave ..." Inhaling the memory, she smiles. "Maybe I'll mention the importance of good scents to Henry."

While waiting for the coffee to brew or the microwave to chirp, compare and contrast your characters' preferences with your own. The better you know your characters the better you propel your readers into their world.

Maybe the prospect of knowing your characters the way a lover or doctor would makes you slightly queasy. The advantage of fiction, though, is that readers need never know how much your characters resemble you or don't. Autobiographical overtones can be as obvious or subtle as you wish. And instead of consuming handfuls of honey-roasted peanuts every time you introduce a character, identify at least one idiosyncratic trait (constantly running fingers over imaginary piano keys). Then both you and your readers view each character as an individual.

For example, Mark Twain's *Huckleberry Finn* always tells the truth. So when he lies to protect his friend Jim, readers notice. Even the minor characters in this novel, like the thieving Duke and King, seem real because the author develops them beyond stereotype. Why not treat all your characters as real human beings, even those who appear in just one paragraph? Any reader that notices you treating your characters like plot devices drifts from the fictional world.

BRAINSTORMING

To transform flat abstractions into the breathing beings of a fictional world, amass about ten times as many characteristics as you need. Then resist the temptation to use all the information you generate. Such background enhances indirectly. Suggest depth rather than squashing readers beneath superfluous detail, which distances them from the story's action. In real life, people know more about their companions than they articulate to themselves or others. Fiction's just the same.

Some writers become familiar with their characters by charting their traits and having such material ready for emergency. For the moment, Georgina substitutes data about her characters for the lucky charm she's yet to find. Do you consider collecting details busy work? Inventing history and temperament breathes life into your characters and sparks ideas for conflict and plot.

Start with the obvious. According to Kurt Vonnegut, "You need a name right away. Otherwise, the character doesn't develop and grow or have much of a personality." (Loretta Leone McCabe in Strickland, 134) After establishing the basics, speculate on the nuances. Naturally, not all writers need all these lists. Alternative techniques can get writers cozy with their characters. What matters is brainstorming enough that you relate to your characters as if they're real. Georgina, of course, insists that fictional characters are.

Character Data Sheet A: Fundamentals

- ❖ Name
- ❖ Age
- ❖ Appearance
- ❖ Occupation
- ❖ Income
- ❖ Education
- ❖ Environment
- ❖ Personal Chronology

- ❖ Hobbies
- ❖ Pet(s)
- ❖ Religion
- ❖ Ethnic Background
- ❖ Class
- ❖ Occupations of Parents and/or Children

Once you set up the basics, go on to probe further.

Character Data Sheet B: Personal Quirks

- Talents
- Dislikes
- Eccentric Habits
- Phobias
- Ability to Change and Grow
- Food Choices
- Favorite Clothing Items
- Color Preferences
- Sound of Laughter
- Reaction to Touch by Strangers
- Shopping Patterns

- Size of Vocabulary
- Aspirations
- Favorite Setting
- Number of Friends
- Drinking Habits
- Feelings about Smoking
- Favorite pain killer
- Method of Handling Change
- Letter Writing Habits
- Storage of Photographs
- Musical Preferences

This second list gets closer to the hearts of people—and characters, moving them beyond stick figures to human beings with heft and substance. Now you're ready for the deepest analysis.

Character Data Sheet C: Privileged Information

- Integrity
- Secrets
- Jealousies
- Animal Totem
- Representative Symbol
- Ugliest Fault
- Most Powerful Memories
- Degree of Resilience
- Problem-Solving Ability

- Means of Coping with Stress
- Method of Defusing Anger
- Resemblance to Real People
- Resonance with Other Characters

Complete some questionnaires or portions of them. Taking the time to print or write up these details makes them more accessible.

Another alternative is a fictional sketch resembling the following example.

"Ted Cody" — by David Berger

Ted Cody lives in a grand fake Tudor house in Lake Forest, the rich, north-shore Chicago enclave. Grew up on the blue-collar south side, changed his name from Teodor Koder. Sneaks out Friday afternoons to play golf at a second-rank country club.

Ted dresses perfectly, gets his clothes at Capper and Capper (the more-prestigious-than-Brooks Brother's men's clothing store). But he slouches when he walks, has rounded shoulders. Became an Episcopalian.

Ted darts away from companions. Walking down the street, he'll say, "Gotta go," and they won't see him again. In the fifth inning at Sox Park with agency guys, he'll disappear and not come back.

Sucks up; kicks down. He speaks to clients from a seated crouch, ducking deeper and deeper to keep his head lower than the client's and thus subservient, as the client slumps deeper and deeper in his high-backed, leather desk chair. Ted kicks Harry in a meeting and, years later, chokes him with two hands around the throat, kidding on the square.

Ted shouts, even screams, in the hall outside his office when challenged on the content of a presentation to a client. Ted and his clients have no agreed-on advertising strategy, which makes writing ads and testing them difficult, and basic research irrelevant. Rather, Ted has a business strategy, which is to find out what the client wants and then sell it to him. Ted is so insincere he doesn't know he's insincere. He does have a guiding principle: The sale is truth.

Ted went to the University of Chicago Business School. He doesn't talk about it because he flunked out.

Yet when Ted tells the story of his try-out with the Detroit Tigers that ended when Tommy Bridges (a great pitcher) threw him curve balls, he's self-deprecating and funny. And when Ted complains to Harry about how tough the business is, and how he's mistreated by an ex-client and by his and Harry's boss, Harry's contempt for Ted is mixed with sympathy.

Note the precision, the glimpses of character in scene, and the combination of repugnant and vulnerable characteristics. Like a real person, Ted exhibits substance and complexity. Novelists, especially, benefit from composing portraits like this.

Several different strategies can acquaint you with your characters. Writer and teacher Marshall Cook visualizes his characters responding to a series of *what ifs*. Could your protagonist survive if abandoned in the desert? What if a happily married character gets stranded with an alluring stranger with no hope of rescue before morning? What if a chocoholic physicist learns that cocoa kills brain cells?

The Character Interview

Your characters must live for you before they can live for your readers. Still feel distant from your characters? Confront them with the career world's conquests and fiascoes. The most juvenile or senior character can seek employment or recall attempts to land a job.

Georgina wakes Henry, sleeping late after an evening with friends. "Get up already."

He stares blearily at her. "I was having this wonderful dream about Ashley."

Georgina shrugs. "I'm sure you'll dream of her again. I'll buy you breakfast while you describe landing your first job."

Henry is soon savoring fresh-squeezed orange juice—in silence.

"Okay, Henry, talk. Your first job interview."

He swallows. "Mother drove me downtown, lecturing me about responsibility, carrying one's own weight, making her proud. I was close to tears—and scared she'd notice. She sent me inside by myself. I was petrified! After this terrible time finding the room, a vast face hovered over an even vaster desk. I wanted to hide, but I mumbled out my carefully rehearsed request.

'Young man,' he thundered, 'will you deposit these weeklies safely inside front doors, come rain or shine?'

'Sir. Oh yes.'"

"C'mon, Henry," Georgina mutters. "This isn't good enough for the canned stuff, much less fresh-squeezed juice. You don't sound like a kid; you sound like Oliver Twist! This won't do. Ever lug glass to the recycle center? Sweep the floor in dad's shop?"

Henry pales.

Georgina leans closer. "Did you wash cars or shovel sidewalks?"

He shakes his head. "Our neighborhood..."

"You'll work till I know who you are. Now about those chocolate bars for orchestra..."

Georgina will pester Henry until they concoct a series of stories. After a few restaurant trips she can answer the following questions.

Interview Questions

- Which jobs have you held and for how long?
- Which employment and life experiences pertain to this job?
- Why do you want this job?
- Which strengths can you offer?
- Which weaknesses must you overcome?
- Would you take a job for which you were over-qualified?
- How quickly can you train?
- What do you like best and least about this job?
- What work-related difficulties do you expect? How would you handle them?
- Do you work well with others?
- How do you cope with unpleasant people with whom you must interact?
- How do you interact with authority figures?
- Are you a *self-starter*?
- Will you work evenings? Weekends?
- At which time of day do you work best?
- Describe ideal working conditions.
- Why are you leaving your present employment? (If relevant.)
- How long do you intend to remain in this job?

ORIGINATING ROUND CHARACTERS

Questionnaires and interviews can generate characters that combine universal traits with individual idiosyncrasies. If your characters still seem flat, treat them to dinner. This can prove costly, though only in terms of time. They can't rack up a bill. Imagine your characters in various restaurants to observe what they want and need— not just what you want and need for them.

Wining and dining your characters needn't parallel the actual plot of your fiction. In fact, unrelated adventures sometimes reveal the most. If you imagine your characters in situations associated with your fiction, you learn more about plot. Want to learn more about character? Picture your characters in situations irrelevant to your plot. For example, in a novel about scientists introducing terrestrial life to a recently discovered barren planet, escort the specialists to a Mississippi

McDonald's back on earth. Burgers could be extinct by then, but force fast food down your biologists anyway. Would they dislike unfamiliar, fat-laced scents and flavors? Would they debate the political correctness of beef and cholesterol?

Don't just analyze. Mentally film your characters interacting in a setting. Where does everyone sit? What do the scientists think of those ridiculous hats and aprons? One visit may not reveal enough. Your team works its way through pizza, tacos, more burgers, and finally, dinner theatre. By the time you're done, you know how your characters hold their knives and forks. You can imagine what happens when the protagonist drops something on the floor or drips something down a shirtfront. Once you can visualize several situations, you have your characters when you need them.

Identity

Names cement the impression that characters have three dimensions, unlike shapes children cut from cardboard. To create the illusion of reality, fictional characters must seem more consistent yet subtle than their real-life counterparts. Consider names. Parents choose *Robert* or *Henrietta* without foreknowledge. Writers, though, can name their *children* to suggest geography, social status, hopes, and dreams. To illustrate, Wallace Stegner's characters in *Angle of Repose* include the helpful *Ada* and fragile *Shelley* of the watchful *Hawkes* family. Stegner's cast also includes the second-in-command Frank *Sargent*, the haughty *Augusta*, and the rationalizing *Lyman* of the preservationist *Ward* lineage. None of these names necessarily attract attention. Many readers never notice symbolism contributing on the subtlest of levels. Yet in this Pulitzer Prize-winning novel, names reinforce character.

Few writers incorporate symbolism the way Stegner does. Yet names do matter. Choosing *Robert Allen Smith* could send readers after a more interesting protagonist, while the moniker *Prudence Wingspan* introduces levity. Choose names that reinforce your intentions without distracting. Unless the circumstances involve parental fondness for alliteration, don't christen siblings *Ellen, Elizabeth,* and *Edward.*

Universal and Singular

Naming characters initiates their identity, the first step in creating beings that seem both typical and representative. This helps readers accept characters as real. In the genre of traditional melodrama, readers expect to encounter a hero, a villain, and a distressed damsel. Today, characters like these seem flat and stereotypical (a version of *unreal),* because readers only know who deserves sympathy. In contrast, even the "villains" of contemporary fiction demonstrate human moments, and strawberry blondes now lead battalions to victory. Complicate stereotypes with individual traits and composite emotions, such as pain and jealousy accompanying anger.

Credible characters both convince and surprise. Unite universal, familiar traits (such as liking Friday Fish Fry and dreading Monday email) with distinctive ones (such as arriving by 6:30 a.m. to deal with all those Monday messages). Vital, breathing beings emerge from combining eccentricities with generalities.

Some writers dole out one or two inclinations or mannerisms at a time, just as new encounters provide additional enlightenment in real life.

"Hey," Georgina asks Patsy, "can you introduce me to that cute guy with the crooked smile? The one who spent most of your party in the kitchen?"

They meet. Cute Guy reveals that he travels the world investigating volcanic activity.

Three weeks later Georgina tells Patsy, "Not sure I'm still interested. He doesn't own any furniture. Lives out of cartons. Always keeps carrots in the fridge—nothing else. Guess he needs good eyes to decipher the labels on all those boxes."

Georgina gives Cute Guy one last chance. When she learns that he loathes cats, she requires no further information.

Gradual disclosure of detail suggests realism and builds suspense.

REVEALING CHARACTERS

Many techniques can flesh out characters. Consider combining strategies. You can show them through what they do or say as well as what others say about them. When necessary, the narrator can tell what you can't otherwise show.

Behavior

Character conflict, external or internal, efficiently reveals character. Compare and contrast reactions to a flood, for example. How will individuals confront loss, rage, fear, and perhaps hunger? Make certain, though, that your characters have options. Watching helpless characters intrigues readers no more than watching uneventful, perfect lives.

When characters face reasonable odds, then their choices, behavior, and ability to grow can reveal temperament. Showing characters reacting to adversity requires more words and effort. Contrast these examples:

> Everyone disliked Mrs. Henderson's bossy arrogance.
>
> *Versus*
>
> Irene tried to slink past Mrs. Henderson.
> "Irene!"
> "Er, yes, ma'am."
> "Have you typed the reports I asked you to complete before lunch?"
> "Not yet, I ..."
> "Unbelievable. When I was in your position, I accomplished my tasks expediently. When my superiors relied on me, I provided ..."
> "Uh, yes ma'am. I'm right on it."
> Outside, Irene met Helen's gaze and rolled her eyes.

Which example puts Mrs. Henderson right in the reader's face? Presenting characters in scenes eliminates the need to tell.

Habits also disclose character. For example, an executive exposes her anxiety by constantly checking whether bra straps are tucked inside her blouse. An ex-smoker holds his fingers as if a cigarette burned there. An adolescent flexes his arm to check whether his biceps have grown during the last ten minutes.

Dialogue

Like habits, conversation between characters can provide insight into personality and involve readers directly.

"HONestly, mom, I don't need you in the dressing room with me."

"You don't. I see. Then how can I know whether I think these things look good on you?"

"Easy, MOTHer. It doesn't matter whether you think it looks good."

"I see. Even though I'm paying."

"Oh, man, I can't stand this! Why must we go through this every time!"

"Because I pay every time. Until you're ready to change that, I'll just have a look."

"Oh, okay, if you have to. But don't you dare tell anyone you came in the dressing room with me. If you do, I'll just die."

"Well, we wouldn't want that, would we."

Without much description, readers can discern the approximate age of the daughter, her embarrassment over her friends realizing that she has a mother, and the mother's response to an evidently chronic syndrome. This conversation depicts how the mother and daughter are both typical and singular.

Character Comments

Revealing characters exclusively through action and dialogue can prove formidable. So writers often use what characters say about each other.

Such a shame about Fred Robbie retiring. This new principal, Howard Nelson, seems fine, though a little intent on having things his way. He invites me to make an appointment to get acquainted, then immediately points out I came three minutes late. I didn't bother apologizing, just smoothed down the hem of my skirt, demurely crossed my ankles, and changed the subject. You know, school policy. I thought he should hear how we've handled things.

For instance, I informed him that Fridays teachers never stay past three. He gives me this look, like how's Friday different from any other day? So, I offer my sweetest smile and remind him how much work all of us take home weekends. He just stares, doesn't return my smile, and points to the line in the contract about hours in the building. Imagine! Why Fred Robbie'd no more wave a contract in my face than he'd shoot me. This principal seems to think he's the best thing to hit education since the blackboard. Maybe he should remember that some of us have been running this school since before he was born. Fred Robbie knew that, knew it for sure.

This portrait establishes a great deal about the new principal. He believes in meeting with staff ("invites me to make an appointment to get acquainted"), watches the clock ("points out I came three minutes late"), upholds written agreements and their details ("points to the line in the contract about hours in the building"), and isn't easily charmed ("doesn't return my smile").

Characters also reveal themselves through what they divulge deliberately or inadvertently. This veteran teacher discloses her own personality along with Howard Nelson's. She shows up late for her first appointment with him, considers herself ladylike ("demurely crossed my ankles"), and relies on her ability to charm ("offer him my sweetest smile").

The narrator begins with neutral comments ("Howard Nelson seems fine") but then hints at some unsubstantiated conclusions; the new principal seems difficult ("a little intent on having things his way") and condescending ("seems to think he's the best thing to hit education since the blackboard"). She assumes her right to power ("some of us have been running this school since before he was born") and voices frustration about the altered status quo ("such a shame about Fred Robbie retiring"). Readers infer that she wrapped Fred around her little finger. This narrator reveals as much about herself as Howard Nelson.

Authorial Comment

Finally, writers can describe character, though without telling more than necessary. Direct revelation works best in situations fused with tension, as this dinner party illustrates.

> He stood silent, amazed that she'd belittle him in front of guests they hardly knew. No matter how often he reconstructed things in his head, their marital roles stayed stable. He'd sell his soul if asked. After all these years he couldn't seem to change that, while she treated him like a dog. A very bad dog. Like most dog owners, if she considered her pet naughty, she didn't much care if others overheard her scold him or not.

In some cases, summarizing a pattern can be more effective than detailing recurrent conversations or incidents that demonstrate the same tendency.

INTEGRATING STRATEGIES

Most fiction, however short, develops character through more than one approach. A combination of techniques adds dimension to the characters in the following sketch.

"The Cookie Chairman" — by Melissa Paton

"All right, ladies, line up facing me."

In our drab-brown uniforms, fifteen of us scrambled to a line on the gym floor. It seemed like a promising start—could be the beginning of a Red Rover game.

Mrs. Lokken began pacing in front of us. "Girls, I'm very disappointed. Cookie sales are down from last year. Troop 137 is way ahead of us, and we just can't lose our place as top regional sellers. Everyone is going to have to pull together and sell, sell, sell."

No problem, I thought. I'll have Dad take some more to the office. He did a really good job selling the last bunch.

"It seems like everyone is moving thin mints, but we have a lot more varieties. We've got an overload of shortbread cookies. Everyone's going to take three cases home tonight and have them sold by the next meeting. No excuses."

No problem. I have three aunts in town who are always willing to buy whatever I sell. I can have those cases sold with three quick phone calls.

"And some of you, we won't mention names, have yet to sell their first case. What kind of outfit do you think we are? You Brownies need to get out there to the grocery stores. Knock on every door in your neighborhood and the neighborhood after that until all of those cookies are out of my garage." Mrs. Lokken was so red she looked like her head was going to pop.

But I felt no worries. I'd sold more than my quota. I could sell more to my relatives. There would be no standing in front of a grocery shivering in my uniform. This was not my problem—until I looked over at my best friend, Sarah Lu Wepner. Her lower lip trembled. Tears filled her eyes. Sarah Lu's dad was a farmer. She had no neighborhood.

I sighed and held back my own tears. I knew my mom would be driving us to the grocery store this weekend.

Behavior, dialogue, and character comment reveal character. Paton contrasts the children's behavior with the adult's: they scrambled and Mrs. Lokken began pacing. Financial concerns ("sell, sell, sell") and competition ("Troop 137 is way ahead of us") make this leader willing to hurt feelings ("some of you, we won't mention names, have yet to sell their first case"). The narrator's comments on the situation ("Sarah Lu's dad was a farmer. She had no neighborhood") disclose that the Brownie's empathy exceeds her leader's. The child's observations substitute for the author intervening to divulge anything more.

DESIGNING CHARACTER DEVELOPMENT

Familiarity with strategies for revealing character helps you eliminate unnecessary characters or events. A preliminary outline, however vague, lets you make more events befall fewer characters.

When Georgina started this novel, she rationalized about needing an overview. "It'd constrain me—defeat spontaneity," she murmured to Cinnamon.

Overhearing this, Henry's mother's summoned the redhead who had imagined her into existence. "My dear! Be sensible." Mrs. Petry waved her finger in Georgina's face. "Consider which you wish to discard. Would that be an outline, a short story or, heaven forbid, an entire novel? And never dream you'll get away with deleting passages that include me."

Humbly, Georgina sets to work planning.

To prevent chucking characters or outlines you worked hard to design, picture a bare plot of land. Successful crops require perhaps five times the space of the original planting. So skillful gardeners determine how much to sow by conceptualizing the space necessary not for the seedlings but the plants ready for harvest. Both gardens and fiction require room to maneuver and pull things together. Introduce your characters as if a tiny tomato seedling will become a large, prolific plant. Tomatoes and marigolds work well together. Interweave new characters by interaction or relationship with those already present.

Balance and Interconnection

Develop characters as parts of a whole. To illustrate, in the world of the three little pigs, the lackadaisical hogs intensify their compulsive brother's righteousness. Influence flows in both directions. Would those party-loving swine behave more responsibly if they deemed their brother reasonable? The interaction between the protagonist and those surrounding the character must resemble a seesaw; individual movements or decisions affect everyone involved. Seesaws require balance. No one wants to play or watch if one participant possesses all the power.

Once all your characters have options, you can pit them against each other. But real people have more than one dimension and often experience more than one conflict at once. To bolster credibility, give the conflict greater depth than the tale of those pigs. Don't oversimplify character inclinations and goals. For example, both selfish and generous people frequently seek the same award, promotion, marriage partner, lifestyle, and the rest. Similar goals evoke similar behavior, even when the protagonist is more compassionate than the antagonist. When you compare characters in light of a noticeable trait or objective, these characters function as foils.

One character can serve as a foil for several others, deepening and clarifying them all. In Harper Lee's *To Kill a Mockingbird,* for example, she contrasts innocence with both haughtiness and cruelty. Self-serving Tom Ewell functions as a foil for gentle, generous, and innocent Boo Radley. If Boo is a mockingbird, then Tom Ewell is a vulture. Scout, Tom Robinson, and to varying degrees other characters represent mockingbirds along with Boo. Not one of Lee's characters exists in a vacuum, and this interconnectedness enhances insight into them all.

Yet Lee doesn't oversimplify her cast into *good* versus *bad* characters. Readers understand why Mayella Ewell unjustly accuses Tom Robinson of rape. Like *To Kill a Mockingbird,* many strong novels suggest a continuum of innocence versus experience, power versus weakness, and other contrasts. To seem lifelike, characters must blend qualities with deficiencies. Maybe a *good* character suffers delusions of grandeur. Perhaps a *bad* one mocks customers yet graciously offers to mow an ailing neighbor's lawn. Knowledge of your characters generates composite portraits that combine capabilities with shortcomings. Once your characters resemble not caricatures but people, you can more easily capture the distinct sound that each one must deliver.

SENDING CHARACTERS INTO THE FICTIONAL WORLD

You've broken bread with your characters, sent them after jobs, and scrutinized their reactions to earthquakes and power outages. After all that, you eavesdropped on their comments about themselves and each other. By now you probably know enough about them to make them real for your readers.

Checklist: Character Revelation

✓   Do you know more about your protagonist than you include?
✓   Do you use more than one strategy to reveal character?
✓   Are your characters credible?
✓   Are your characters familiar yet original?
✓   Do your characters combine universality with individuality?
✓   Does each character mix some *good* with some *bad*?
✓   Can readers reach their own conclusions about your characters?
✓   Do your characters offer some insight into human nature?

STRETCHING EXERCISES

1.   Interview your character.

   Complete a job application for this individual. What kind of job does the character seek? Use the questions in this chapter or make up your own.

2.   Describe your character's physical appearance without telling.

   Convey that a character is tall, underweight, attractive, etc. Use at least one other character to help readers infer some information about clothing, hairstyle, fingernails, and so on.

3.   Take a character to dinner.

   Visualize anything from neighborhood bar to fancy hotel. How would one or more of your characters react to this location? What would they eat? How would they behave?

LOOKING BACK, THEN AHEAD

"Ashley. Ashley!" Georgina mutters to Muffin, "Oh great. One of my main characters is so unclear I can't even conjure her. What so entices Henry?"

Georgina puts the amorphous, ambiguous Ashley through her paces. How would she describe herself? How would she describe Henry? A little nervously, Georgina wonders how Ashley would describe a redhead who writes. Does Ashley like Georgina? Of course she does. Ashley likes everyone.

Ashley begins taking shape. Her cloud of curly blonde hair. Her habit of twirling a long strand around one finger. Georgina sends Ashley out to an interview at the Children's Museum. Ashley would love working there, but not if they make her wear stockings. She's conflicted. Giving people things pleases her, but she can't give much until she improves at supporting herself. Georgina discovers that Ashley's great-grandfather was a country doctor who rode his horse and buggy out to his patients even in the worst blizzards. Credit cards disgust Ashley, though the concept of virtual shopping delights her. Ashley describes herself as a "growing thing"; she can't wait to own a house in order to plant a huge garden. Henry calls her "the most beautiful person he's ever met."

There. Georgina has what Ashley thinks and does as well as how others describe her. She's coming to life. But Georgina hasn't conversed with her yet. How do writers make conversations between characters sound like real people talking?

CHAPTER 3: Dialogue

Simulating Conversational Reality

Dialogue in fiction should be reserved for the culminating moments and regarded as the spray into which the great wave of fiction breaks. (Edith Wharton in Collins, 37- 38)

HANDLING CONVERSATION

Georgina thinks to herself, "Dialogue, schmialogue. Some people are born knowing how to write it. However, I am not one of them." Frowning, she summons her protagonist so that they can talk.

"What is it that you would like to have from me, Georgina?" said Henry to her in his normal tone of voice.

"Henry, I would like at this time to discuss the progress of our book with you," she stated steadfastly and calmly to him.

"Georgina, the present would not be a good time for us to talk," he rejoined facilely but smoothly and determinedly.

"It is momentous that I speak with you right now," Georgina said harshly and hastily with a note of anger in her tone.

"I cannot cooperate with that," Henry said intolerantly.

"Then I do not fathom what I will do," Georgina said plaintively.

Georgina's dialogue definitely needs work. What problems do you detect?

When dialogue sounds credible, it not only serves numerous purposes but also fulfills more than one function at a time.

- Introduce new characters.
- Present exposition.
- Position characters in scene.
- Suggest immediacy.

- Complicate plot.
- Add conflict or foreshadowing.
- Alter atmosphere or tempo.
- Deliver the climax.

Good dialogue can make fiction memorable or laughable. What makes dialogue work?

Verisimilitude

Dialogue must simulate reality. Do you worry that you can neither reproduce conversation nor fabricate it from scratch? Don't feel discouraged; you can develop this skill. Some writers want to record actual exchanges. Perhaps this misconception arises from the realm of biography, where convention prevents authors from imagining what individuals said.

Such restrictions don't curtail fiction writers, who require the simulation of reality. The fiction writer's goal isn't duplicating conversation but providing believable, suspenseful dialogue that suggests authenticity without inflicting the drawbacks of actual speech. Fictional dialogue is selective. Recollecting how many exchanges transpired before people expressed something important or interesting doesn't contribute.

Literal transcription bores readers, because conversations often drag on like this:

> "So, then, how long you been here? Not long, I hope. What time did you come?"
>
> "Oh, I guess I'm not really sure. I don't think I even looked at my watch."
>
> "I see. Ah ha. Well. Then, you don't know...er, what time you arrived. Um, so were you driving a long time, do you think? Uh, run into any construction, roadblocks, or anything?"
>
> "Well, I'm not sure, um, how long it took. No construction though. I can't say what time I left. Could have been right after lunch. Or, come to think of it, could be quite a while after. Maybe not till mid-afternoon. No. Not before, I don't think."
>
> "How you doing then? Everything under control? Nancy doing well? Anything I should know about?"
>
> "Everything's under control. I'm okay; she is, too. We're fine."

However accurate, this conversation feels neither "fine" nor "okay." Protect not your memories but the credibility and charm of your fictional world. Unlike the repetition and circularity of real conversation, characters should speak briefly and interrupt frequently.

Fictional conversation must convince and concern readers. If you want your dialogue to accomplish some purpose, such as introducing a character or conflict, heed your instinctive knowledge of what people share with each other. Readers exit the fictional world once they wonder why a wife reminds her husband that she works in a bank or a son informs his mother of his age. Protect credibility.

Jerome Lawrence, co-author of *Inherit the Wind*, defines verisimilitude as "the *appearance* of truth. But sometimes you want a higher truth; by boiling something down to the essence of it, you may get a higher truth and know that the essence is completely fictional." (Christopher Meeks in Strickland, 68) To reach that "higher truth," dialogue must seem realistic without necessarily capturing reality. The "essence" of conversation involves exchanges about what characters want or need. Trivial verbiage about health, weather, and road conditions doesn't add. Dialogue should reveal dreams, memories, and frustrations.

Conflict

Conversations about dreams and frustrations generate tension. Excessive detail, repetition, or speaker attribution (identifying who says what) diminish reader involvement. The same tautness that pushes scenes forward, however, can render dialogue too fast-paced for credibility. Slow pace also impedes. Hint that the conversation has lagged for some time. Otherwise, you won't convey the "essence" of the interaction. Consider this exchange:

> "Tell me about your day."
> "Fine, thanks. You?"
> "Not bad. Know what you want for supper?"
> "No, what do you feel like?"
> "Maybe we could go out."
> "We went out yesterday."
> "Well, yes, of course I know that. But I still don't feel like cooking."

Contrast that interaction with:

> "Hey there." Ralph looked up from the sports section. "So what's for supper?"
> Rubbing the back of her neck, she exhaled, then plunged ahead. "Let's go out."
> "For the third time in three nights?"

This second exchange thrusts readers into the potential explosion. The terse responses imply poor communication. The strategic last line indicates that this struggle recurs and perhaps represents only one issue dividing this couple.

ADDING SUBTEXT

His question about "the third time in three nights" relies on subtext, or the unwritten meaning that readers must infer. The implied or figurative content of this man's message resides in an implicit judgment that he conveys without articulating it. Properly executed, the content of subtext exists so tangibly that readers imagine overhearing actual words. Subtext resonates with reality, because much communication, both within fiction and outside it, relies on inference.

Unspoken words thrust readers into active interpretation of a scene. For example, a woman slams down the phone after speaking with someone at the doctor's office. Talking with her husband later, she never mentions this call. She does tell him that her feet hurt, their checking account's running low, and the cat threw up on the new rug again. Readers wonder. Is the wife pregnant? Not pregnant? Perhaps she's seriously ill? Or he is? Subtext instigates curiosity.

Georgina often reaches for chocolate when she needs to incorporate subtext. "Easy for you, Cinnamon," she accuses. "No messages between the lines for you. Cats just mew out whatever they want to express." She turns on the television, stares at it blankly for a moment, shuts it off. "Henry," she calls, "come here a second, please— if you have time. Did I tell you I'm getting a new keyboard? They said there's too much fur in this one. And the cats have to...nothing new with you, right?"

Henry looks up from the syllabus he's reviewing. "Did you want something, Georgina?"

"Nothing special. I told you about the keyboard and the vet appointment, right? I just wondered. Want to take Ashley for a movie?"

"Absolutely, but there's nothing good."

"Right." Georgina inspects her new chenille bedspread for claw or teeth marks. "A walk by the lake?"

"Sounds good. I'd ask her, but they predict rain. Besides, I don't need a ploy for calling."

"Course not, and weather reports are never wrong."

Henry looks out his window. "Wrong often enough, but not today. Dark clouds. Gathering. Georgina, did I mention how terrible my allergies are? Could be starting a cold."

"I wouldn't want you sick with the semester starting. You know what's best! Weren't you going to ask Ashley about that herb? The one that doesn't cause drowsiness?"

"I thought about it, but mom's doctor friend insists it's a bad idea. You know I want to do this, Georgina. When the time's right, I will."

"That makes sense, Henry. And I know you always take your mom's advice."

Henry shrugs, then heads to the medicine cabinet for two aspirin.

This interaction circles around the issues troubling Georgina and Henry, issues that neither of them articulates.

Georgina must want Henry to ask Ashley out or Georgina wouldn't suggest a film, a walk, and a pretext for calling. Yet Georgina won't tell Henry what to do, perhaps from concern that her advice will backfire. Henry reveals ambivalence. These suggestions "sound good." Ultimately though, he acts only on his headache.

If Georgina confronts Henry about his insecurity, this generates tension, as arguments do. Yet such a passage can't provide the excitement of uncovering what the characters express beneath pleasantries about movies and weather. If Georgina thinks Henry can make his own decisions, she'd never say "you know what's best." Henry must feel defensive, or he wouldn't insist that he doesn't "need a ploy for calling." Showing encourages reader participation.

PACING DIALOGUE

Details like the protagonist rinsing the salad while starting an argument control the momentum of character conversation. Pace involves how much tension develops and how rapidly it escalates. You can temporarily diminish intensity with someone stroking a hand-made quilt or glaring at the squirrels emptying the bird feeder. Such details position characters in physical space and modulate tempo.

When theatre people describe the actions that accompany speech, they call it *stage business*. In fiction, stage business can delay the moment when readers discover the answer to a crucial question. A detail such as the sun streaming through the window onto the character's bald scalp divides dialogue into more digestible morsels and helps readers visualize the scene and identify the speaker. If a couple fights during breakfast, the husband can spear his bacon before it escapes unpunished, while his wife fantasizes splashing coffee on him as she refills his cup. In response to the clattering dishes, their Pekinese slinks down to the basement. Intersperse dialogue with stage business.

Don't tell those details. "Margaret chomped off the end of her hangnail, watching the blood ooze off the edge of her finger" rather than "Margaret couldn't control her self-destructive habits." But balance description with conversation. Use stage business too often, and it sounds artificial or renders dialogue bumpy or sluggish. Curtail the number and duration of such delays, and don't insert interruptions that readers will resent. A heated exchange between mother and son is not the moment to determine the value of the Ming vases on the mantel. Pauses in dialogue seem most legitimate when they fulfill more than one purpose, such as slowing the pace while revealing character, developing symbolism, foreshadowing the future, or identifying the speaker.

CHOOSING TO SAY OR NOT TO SAY

Carefully timed interruptions help clarify speaker attribution, or identification, without repeating *he said, she said, he said* unnecessarily. You've probably heard warnings about overusing the past participle *said.* Yet distracting substitutions for this overly maligned verb manufacture worse problems. Better repeat *said* than insert inexact synonyms that perplex readers. Many synonyms for *said* succeed in terms of denotation but not connotation. Unless your character is lecturing, repeat the word *said* instead of assaulting readers with the heavy-handed *expostulated.* Only in special circumstances can you use *stated, uttered, queried, interrogated, conversed, affirmed, pronounced, annunciated, asserted,* or *declared.* Don't identify speaker with verbs unrelated to speech, such as *yawned, shuddered, tittered, ogled, pleased, disrupted, gulped, swooned,* or *smiled.*

An alternative either to *said* or its synonyms is attributing speaker about one-third of the time. Dividing the conversations into thirds isn't necessary or appropriate! Assess the passage to determine the moment when readers wonder who is talking. Consider the voices in this example:

"Let's review the plan. We check our list, find the items we discussed, get in line. Nothing else. Agreed?"

"Oh ma, you're always...yeah, yeah, no computer games. Guess so."

"Yes, mommy, I promise. But Kim's mom said she got to pick one extra thing. I'd like it to do that."

"Just the list."

"Hey, lookit them pants. They are way cool."

"It's not fair. If he gets new pants, then I get the dragonfly pin. Kim has ..."

"Neither of you will get any of those things. Remember the list. School supplies only."

"What if I trade all those stupid folders for new pants? The dumb teachers ..."

"Don't talk about your teachers that way. I've told you again and again not to ..."

"He called teachers *dumb*! How come he gets to use bad words and get new pants but I can't even have a hairpin when Kim and Margie and Erica ..."

"Be quiet! The list. Focus now, please."

"Who wants all this junk anyways? They make us buy stuff we don't need. Or if we do it's in the locker when we're in homeroom, and if we're at our locker they doan say we need it, so ..."

"One more word and we're out of this store without buying a thing!"

The more the dialogue reflects character idiosyncrasies, the less identification you need to provide. You can clarify speaker attribution through one or more of the following:

1. Speech patterns ("check our list"; "just the list"; "the list")
2. Behavioral patterns ("Kim's mom said")
3. Concrete items ("the pants")
4. Distinctive voices ("lookit," "anyways," "they doan say")

Vary how you indicate who delivers each line.

SUGGESTING INDIVIDUALITY

Interviewing, dining, and wining your characters helps unearth their singular sounds. If you get stuck in one voice, try assuming a different physical position as you capture various characters. To develop one voice, sit at the kitchen table. For another voice, lie down on your bed. Movement from one location to another can remind you to enter another head and generate a different sound. So can changing your attire.

To stock up on a variety of hats, Georgina visited a thrift store. Sometimes, when she wants to hear Henry, she slips on a baseball cap and calls him. In barely audible tones, he assures her that he's not procrastinating about Ashley, only awaiting the ideal moment. Georgina nods, tosses the cap across the room, tucks her hair behind her ears, and inhales. "Time for Mrs. Petry." To grasp that voice, Georgina sorts through the hat collection a second time, selecting a Jackie Kennedy pillbox in shocking pink. Georgina secures the hat on her head, then looks Mrs. Petry straight in the eye. "Okay. Henry's lack of ambition. Tell me all about it."

Although the Petry son and mother share a slight Bronx accent, their voices are otherwise distinct. Identifying a sound for each character, inserting viable synonyms for *said*, and adding stage business like Samantha kept biting her lip until Mrs. Eggers wondered whether the child would start bleeding help maintain conversational flow without frustrating readers over who says what.

PRODUCING A NATURAL SOUND

Readers assume that in private life even the stuffiest professionals resemble other folks. Even unusually formal people in an unusually formal setting, such as diplomats nibbling hors d'oeuvres at the Ritz, must sound more natural than stiff. Your goal is verisimilitude, in this case suggesting the flavor of conversation rather than actual particulars.

Checklist: Conversational Sound

✓ Adopt a casual, colloquial tone. *(*"My day was great" *not* "My day was euphoric.")

✓ Use contractions unless you have good reason not to. ("I won't go" *not* "I will not be going," except when characters are upset, strait-laced, or seeking special emphasis.)

✓ Reproduce conversational grammar. ("It's me" *not* "It is I.")

✓ Simulate pauses. ("She toyed with her spoon" or interruptions like "so" *not* "uh," "um," "well," "er," "hmm.")

✓ Abbreviate exchanges. ("You coming?" *not* "Are you coming?")

Use interruptions, pauses, and colloquial language or style to shape convincing, reasonably paced dialogue. Readers prefer brief, intense interactions to long stretches of conversation that lack immediate drama.

MANAGING DIALECT

Readers can't experience drama if difficulty interpreting the language distances them from character and action. Use dialect sparingly and only when integral to characterization, plot, or theme. Literal transcription of speech patterns forces readers to translate fictional passages into a familiar language. Who wants to spend twice as much time in order to eke out the sounds or reconstruct the grammar? Evaluate the readability of the following:

> Ven vee fust cum to thees shores, vee vant to makes a hum vor our jung vuns. Vee says to ourselfs, "Vy iss ete sech uh hardships tuh leaf behind vut ve knew ven vhut ve vant ve kin picture so clear?"

Perhaps this accurately represents immigrant dialect, but few readers want to struggle with many pages like this. To confirm how taxing dialect can seem, revisit one of Jim's monologues from the novel many consider among America's greatest. In *Huckleberry Finn*, Jim's speech evokes Mark Twain's own saying about a classic being "a book which people praise and don't read," in this instance, because readers dislike deciphering material that resembles an unknown language.

Difficult dialect can bury the storyline. Simulation, however, works wonders. Selected phrases can capture a character's uniqueness and suggest that dialect flavors every word. For example, one character might change some but not all *w* sounds to *v*. Instead of altering a succession of letters, a character can add *r* to words like idea or omit the *h* from *thing*. In representative examples, an individual can drop a letter like *g* (*showin'* or *showin* versus *showing*), reflect regional pronunciation (*sahndwhich* or *mhawth*). As Frank McCourt's work demonstrates, the goal is suggestion rather than accurate representation.

Be equally sparing with grammatical errors or regional colloquialisms, such as, "Now we teach you this lesson," or "We're likely to go rowing this afternoon, hey?" Let readers keep moving. Awareness of pacing helps you intuit how often to add unfamiliar language and grammar.

SHOWING VERSUS TELLING

Credible, well-paced dialogue illustrates character emotion and motivation. Refrain from editorializing. Sometimes, though, concerned that readers will miss the point, writers tack on a clarifying adverb (a modifier usually ending in *ly*), such as she sneered *saucily*. Yet each instance of telling interrupts reader participation in the fictional world. Moreover, telling readers that characters uttered the words *furiously* or whispered them *wittily* irritates readers that don't find the remarks *furious*, *witty*, or whatever the hopeful writer labeled them. Don't resort to short cuts and quick fixes. Let readers infer from dialogue and its subtext.

Contrast the following exchanges:

> She hated it when her stupid brother messed with her stuff. "Be quiet," she said angrily!
>
> "Sorry," he stated nastily. What was the big deal? Why did she always have to get mad and yell at him like that, he thought brazenly!
>
> Enraged, she thought to herself, "He never cares about my privacy! He's probably broken something else of mine, like always." She shouted up the stairs with violent rage, "Mom. Mom! He was in my jewelry box again." Then she hollered at her kid brother with fury, "Get out of my sight!"

This passage tells how to interpret character feelings. Unless writers let readers imagine something, why read fiction? Characters can reveal their emotions without writers explaining or relying on exclamation points. Within angry dialogue, emphatic punctuation contributes.

Attached to speaker attribution, however, emphatic punctuation commands readers to notice something.

How do minor changes affect the preceding conversation?

> She glared at her little brother. "Shut up! How many times must I tell you not to mess with my stuff?"
> "Sorry." How he wanted to figure out what attached the clasp to that second thingamajig.
> "You sure don't sound sorry. Look at this. You broke it, you stupid jerk! Mom, mom, he messed with my jewelry again and ruined my best bracelet. Get out of my sight, you pathetic little creep!"

Here the characters reveal themselves. However, you can undermine that effect by telling after you show, as this next example demonstrates:

> "Shut up!" I yelled at my kid brother who, just for a change, was ticking me off! "How many times must I tell you not to mess with my stuff!" I was so mad I couldn't see straight.
> "Sorry." His face was twisted into a nasty sneer, like he didn't even hear me.
> "You sure don't sound sorry." I glowered at him, searching for a way to make him understand how he infuriated me, how I couldn't stand him! "Look at this! You broke it, you stupid jerk!" I had to tell mom all the things he did to make me mad. "Mom, mom, he messed with my jewelry again and ruined my best bracelet. Get out of my sight, you pathetic little creep!" I roared at him, unable to stand his being anywhere near me.

Without explanation, yes, maybe some readers will miss the point. Offending through overstatement, however, involves a greater risk.

Good dialogue tells no more than necessary, as this passage from Jane Austen's *Mansfield Park* illustrates. A poor cousin informs her benefactor, Sir Thomas, that she has rejected the wealthy but unscrupulous Henry Crawford. Sir Thomas demands Fanny's response to her suitor's accusation that she misled him. Fanny replies,

> "How could Mr. Crawford say such a thing? I gave him no encouragement yesterday—On the contrary, I told him—I cannot recollect my exact words—but I am sure I told him that I would not listen to him, that it was very unpleasant to me in every respect, and that I begged him never to talk to me in that manner again.—I am

sure I said as much as that and more; and I should have said still
more if I had been quite certain of his meaning anything seriously;
but I did not like to be,—I could not bear to be—imputing more than
might be intended. I thought it might all pass for nothing with *him*."

[Fanny] could say no more; her breath was almost gone.

"Am I to understand," said Sir Thomas, after a few moments'
silence, "that you mean to *refuse* Mr. Crawford?"

"Yes, Sir."

"Refuse him?"

"Yes, Sir."

"Refuse Mr. Crawford! Upon what plea? For what reason?"

"I—I cannot like him, Sir, well enough to marry him." (659-60)

Much subtext underlies the actual words. Fanny never articulates how
much this proposal mortifies her. Sir Thomas never vocalizes his
contempt for Fanny discarding what he considers her sole chance for
financial security. Austen never states that Sir Thomas terrifies Fanny,
yet not enough to ruin her life because he commands it. Nor does
Austen describe Sir Thomas as cruel, self-centered, and more obsessed
with Fanny's portfolio than her happiness. Yet the words beneath the
words illuminate character feelings. This young woman is determined
to protect her values, while her so-called protector is contemptuous of
her presumption that she can do so.

LETTING DIALOGUE SPEAK FOR ITSELF

Contemporary fiction usually involves more action than novels like
Austen's. Among other reasons, however, readers cherish Austen for
her ability to disappear behind her characters. You, too, must let
readers hear not your voice but those of your characters. Readers will
feel more grateful still if you let them discern nuances that you imply.
Dialogue works when subtext conveys conflict and character voices
echo rather than reproduce reality.

Checklist: Dialogue

✓ Does your dialogue imitate actual conversation?
✓ Do you suggest slang, dialect, jargon, and the rest?
✓ Does your dialogue sound natural?
✓ Do you identify the speaker only often enough for clarity?
✓ Do you vary methods of speaker attribution?
✓ Do you reveal conflict through subtext?
✓ Are exchanges well paced?
✓ Does the dialogue reveal character and/or further plot?

STRETCHING EXERCISES

1. Convey character through spoken interaction.

    Let one character unveil another. Devise a scene where readers experience conversation as if watching not a still frame but a motion picture.

2. Generate dialogue that expresses anger through subtext.

    Make your characters communicate through the words beneath the lines.

3. Take one or two characters to a restaurant where the service is poor.

    Generate dialogue between the manager and one or two of your characters. What does the manager say? What response does this elicit?

LOOKING BACK, THEN AHEAD

To explore the intersection between character and plot, Georgina once deliberately composed a static character portrait. Want to try it? Withstand the temptation to let your character do a single thing. You can delineate height, weight, and hair color along with temperature and climate. Generate more and more description. But nothing can happen—nothing at all. Don't let the character feel, want, or do anything. Maintain that motionlessness. Like Georgina, you may find this unbearable before long.

Georgina evaluates her reaction to the experiment. "Cinnamon, a frozen character sketch is like detaching from time while remaining trapped in a fixed moment. You and I can stare at each other, but we can't blink or move. Ugh! I'll never make my readers feel like this. I swear it! Reminds me of how you freeze when I press you against my chest and deposit kiss after kiss. Ugh again, huh?"

Without conflict, readers can feel as trapped as Cinnamon. Fiction writers generate viable conflict from knowing the characters well enough to understand their feelings and predict their behavior. Without character, plot barely exists. And insubstantial characters seldom produce life-like fiction. Plot that befalls stick figures involves readers no more than viable characters that never act.

Imagine a film opening with a chase scene. Cars occupied by unknown passengers pursue each other through heavy traffic. Unless you know these characters or why they chase each other, you feel like you missed the opening moments. After flat characters drive and shoot for a while, you either want to meet fleshed-out individuals or do something (anything!) else.

In effective fiction, plot and characterization interact. Credible characters face meaningful difficulties that they can theoretically surmount. As they accomplish this, character sketches become fiction. The concept of plot once drove Georgina to her candy stash. Now, familiarity with her characters helps her unravel their conflicts and consume fewer chocolate bars. Still, one question returns over and over. How do you get and keep your characters moving?

CHAPTER 4: Plot Elements

Drafting Reality

Character is destiny. (Heraclitus, in Evans, 95)

CONSTRUCTING A PLAN

Georgina rereads chapter two. "So far so good." She tries to smile. What does Henry do next? He can't ask Ashley out unless... Frowning, she stows her laptop away, looks outside, takes her laptop back out, turns it off. What should she wear tomorrow? Glaring at her closet, she notices the gold patent leather shoes—with pointy toes—bought at a garage sale. For luck. For writing luck. Would Henry...Lots of traffic, she muses. Georgina turns the laptop on, off, glowers, hits reset. Did she finish those peanut clusters?

"Henry!" she hollers into space. "Want to eat out somewhere?"

Her protagonist doesn't respond.

"What would you like to do? I want you to do something! Now!"

Her room looks like empty, narrow space. Nothing more.

"Some thanks I get," Georgina informs Muffin. "You invent these characters, you take them to dinner, then they just...do whatever they want. Sometimes they want to do nothing!"

Muffin rears back.

"Sorry, didn't mean to shout. We'll get past this."

Gingerly at first, Muffin rolls onto his back. Georgina pets him patiently and thoroughly until he stretches toe to toe. Opening his eyes, he studies Georgina with something resembling a smile. Georgina smiles back. She's got lucky writing shoes now.

Perhaps, like Georgina, you treat your characters to meal after meal. You consider yourself intimate with your fictional world and its inhabitants. But readers crave not only characters; readers want characters in motion. If you abandon your creations to their own devices, sometimes they merely breathe, read, and pause to sniff the roses. The writer—not the characters—must assume responsibility for believable and intriguing struggles. Such complications usually require planning and effort.

You can initiate struggle by plunging at least one well-drawn character into trouble. If you develop characters more easily than conflicts, this trouble-making approach produces decisions, if not overt action. Troubled characters can jumpstart your plot. William Faulkner observed that, "With me a story usually begins with a single idea or memory or mental picture. The writing of the story is simply a matter of working up to that moment, to explain why it happened or what caused it to follow." (Winokur, 34) Wondering how to reach that moment?

BUILDING A PLOT

The choice and ordering of events in a narrative comprises its plot. What we call a story (Jane marries Dick) is less specific than a plot, because plot involves the background, incidents, feelings, and interactions leading to Dick and Jane marrying. People associate plot with a linear enactment of events. For fiction writers, however, causality matters: not just *a* and then *b* and *c*, but the relationship between these. Did *a* affect *b* and then *c*? Would *b* to *a* to *c* formulate a more vital or meaningful sequence?

The relationships between *a*, *b*, and *c* form the classic plot structure that most people learned in school. Plot also entails character needs (context, conflict) and character tactics (reactions, behavior) versus their circumstances (advantages, complications). These result in character victory or defeat (climax, outcome).

Blueprint for Structure

Plot involves these elements:

Explosion: A dramatic moment, event, or difficulty that immediately intrigues readers.

Conflict: Character versus self, someone, or something.

Exposition:	Background information so that readers view characters in context.
Storyline:	The events or decisions the main character encounters from the beginning to the end, starting at or just before the conflict.
Complication:	One or more difficulties blocking character progress toward some goal or resolution.
Transition:	Image, symbol, dialogue, or other device used to join each scene, paragraph, or description with what follows.
Flashback:	A return to events prior to the storyline. (optional)
Delay:	Material that temporarily interrupts the storyline, thus building tension.
Climax:	The moment when the conclusion becomes inevitable.
Falling Action:	The slacking off after the climax. (optional)
Resolution:	The solution to the conflict or difficulty within character, community, or environment. (optional)

In constructing your own blueprint for plot, you can either identify these elements or just keep them in mind.

The following plot scheme for Peter Pan combines the J.M. Barrie play with the Walt Disney reconstruction.

A crash through the nursery window wakens Wendy and her brothers John and Michael Darling. (*explosion*) Nana the Nursemaid cares deeply for her Darlings yet has limited abilities. After all, she's a dog responsible for irrepressible children who dream a world more sensational than their own. The uninvited guests who smashed the window arrived from such a world. Peter Pan and Tinkerbell, his magical companion, were enjoying an evening fly when Peter lost his shadow. (*exposition*) Maternal Wendy sews it back on. Grateful Peter teaches all three children to fly, and Tink sprinkles them with fairy dust for their journey to Never Never Land. (*storyline*)

It's a sensational world all right, although thick with problems. (*transition) from England to Never Never Land)* The Lost Boys who live with Peter desperately need mothering. Once they meet Wendy, they want to keep her forever, but she has strong ties to England. (*conflict*) Inside Peter's home everyone is safe (*transition* from hideout to outside world) from vengeful Captain Hook and the buccaneers that threaten Peter and his friends. (*storyline*) Captain Hook holds Peter responsible for a crocodile snatching the Captain's hand. (*exposition*) Will the children escape the pirates? (*conflict*) If Wendy and her brothers remain, what about Nana and the loving Darlings back home? Wendy feels torn. (*conflict*) One restless night she dreams of the lullaby her mother sang. (*flashback*)

Peter's affection for Wendy makes Tinkerbell jealous (*conflict*), and she hopes to make Wendy disappear. Tink's machinations deliver both the fairy and her supposed rival into Captain Hook's hands. Tinkerbell attempts escape and suffers a serious wound. (*complication*) In the past Tink and Peter have often quarreled, especially over Wendy. (*complication*) But Tink's absence makes Peter frantic. (*transition* from one sense of loss to another)

In fact, Peter, Tinkerbell, Wendy, her brothers, and the Lost Boys all miss someone or something. (*conflict*) Even Peter, unwilling to grow up, imagines a less adventurous life. (*delay*) While the kids daydream, the pirates capture everyone except Peter. Tink weakens. She'll survive only if those who believe in fairies clap their hands. (*storyline*) The audience's expression of faith empowers everyone. Peter rescues his pals, drives off the pirates, and Tink recovers! (*climax*) The immediate danger has ebbed, but who will return to England? (*falling action*) Everyone. After all, what good is never growing up if you must do it without a mother? (*resolution*)

Writers control both the events of a scenario like this and the order of relating them. But chronological sequence sometimes lacks vitality. Choose an order that dramatizes the protagonist's difficulties.

PROVIDING AN OPENING

For the same reason, begin with the action of the fiction—not before. This sounds obvious. However, writers frequently present background details at a leisurely pace. Contextual material, referred to as *backstory*, involves information preceding the conflict that drives fiction. Narrative outside the world of fiction, such as anecdotes shared among friends, often depends on backstory. People accept this in conversation, but backstory slows fiction. Plunge into Caroline's anxiety over entering the dorm her first day of college and not the suitcases coming down from the closet, the packing, the lugging to the car, the purchase of gas and perusal of the road map, and other details. After all, what matters is Caroline's first look at her new roommate—who could make even a kid brother seem charming.

Place the protagonist's troubles at center stage. Whatever disturbs the daily pattern provides a sense of action. This is your starting point. Discarding your opening paragraphs often lets readers begin with the story rather than before it.

Georgina stares openmouthed at Mrs. Petry. "Cut most of my first page?"

Mrs. Petry raises one eyebrow. "The real story begins with your fourth paragraph. Dear."

"Don't *dear* me, you ..."

"The advantage to living in your room is overhearing everything you think. I know how you view me. I also know you realize that I'm right. Start with that fourth paragraph."

Cutting hurts. Sometimes you can intersperse that material elsewhere. Otherwise, grit your teeth and confess that you never needed those details after all.

Options for Introducing Plot Elements

The following possibilities can help plunge readers into a fictional world. But the magic comes from the writer—not the technical device.

Conflict: Struggle for resolution or satisfaction.

Tubes came from his mouth, chest, and who knew where else. I can't believe he'd allow that if he could protest. And all I had to do was move one an inch or so to the side. Wouldn't he want that?

Flashback: Return to the past.

"Attention, attention. Flight 1802 is delayed two more hours. Fog over the airport ..."

The night I met Liz, fog filled the air like a curtain separating me from the shadows ahead. She became the one shape I could decipher in the thick air.

Monologue: Commentary from the narrator.

I weighed 90 pounds by the time I was eight. That didn't stop my wanting to be a ballet dancer when I grew up. Every day I'd ask my mom about taking lessons, offering to deliver newspapers or something to pay for them. Her answer never changed, but I never stopped asking. Only later did I realize those conversations were my dance lessons.

Observation: Dramatic statement.

Cancer changes everything.

Environmental Context: The significance of the setting.

The smooth walls of a spacecraft look one way when you're training, quite another when they become the boundaries of your world for who knows how many days, months, years.

Character Context: Character in relation to setting.

Her fingernails never got clean. Winters she spent long days in the greenhouse, always worrying that cold would seep in and get the orchids. The orchids didn't dirty her nails. The ferns did, and the few annuals she couldn't bear to relinquish the night frost hit.

Character Revelation: Character temperament or motivation.

Alice shakes his leg. "Coffee? Coffee make? Alus, coffee?" She giggles at her private joke until her face reddens. She gulps for air, coughs, shakes his leg again. "Help? Coffee me."

Her father exhales, barely noticing how the smoke teases at Alice's moist eyes.

Dialogue: Conversation between characters.

"Have a drink with me."

"Sure, sure I will. Soon as there's a nuclear blast and the two of us are the only ones left."

Language Hook: Dramatic or poetic phrase.

Artifice and artlessness. Artlessness and artifice. He played with the words, crooned them, saw them on his book cover, nightly drugged himself to sleep with them.

Symbolism: Significance beyond the literal meaning.

She's kept his boots by the cellar steps, muddy the way he left them when he walked out for good.

Question: Speculation about circumstances.

Why do parties scare me?

Exposition: Background material.

No one looked at Mrs. Johns, even when she called on you. But when she told us there'd be no Algebra quiz, I closed the magazine inside my notebook. Her face startled me. Under its powder coating, it looked sickly pale. So Cuba could bomb us. I bet even Charlie Meyers was gonna behave during this practice drill. My trembling fingers stroked the sequin collar of the poodle on my skirt.

PROVIDING BACKGROUND INFORMATION

Got your reader's attention? Good, now explain just enough to clarify the conflict. Readers need exposition. Without understanding the context, they can't grasp the conflict and empathize with the *good guys*. Exposition lets readers feel intrigued rather than confused or left out.

But just spell out what readers must know, and they may wonder where the story went. In many instances, you can't impart facts without some telling. Unlike other aspects of fiction, exposition requires this. If you combine essential information with action, then the telling necessary to set up the storyline becomes legitimate. Providing background differs from not trusting your readers to deduce the right conclusions.

The better you blend exposition, the more involved readers become and remain. Dribble essential details in a few at a time, the way cooks trickle the cream into the sauce. If you dump either dairy product or data, you whip up an unappealing concoction. Instead of inviting readers to share a secret, exposition that attracts attention pleads, commands, or prays that readers enter a fictional world. Everyday life involves tedious but essential sifting through detail; readers turn to fiction for the fantasy that they already know all about character, relationship, and environment.

Maintain that illusion. Otherwise, exposition seems tedious or artificial, especially when you plant dialogue intended to convey information. Note the effect of a wife saying, "You've been ordering me about for the last five of the thirty-eight years we've been married." Consider her husband countering with, "I'm not ordering you about, and don't you need your jacket on this chilly Eau Claire evening in 1979?" Dialogue can position characters in time and space but must mirror the kind of information that people share in normal conversation.

> He looked out at the poplars twisting in the wind. "Want your jacket? It's awfully cold for July."
> "When you get tired of ordering me about, let me know. I'm sick of your treating me like a child." She eyed her jacket, then straightened her shoulders and left it on its peg. "This isn't unusual for a Wisconsin evening."
> "Suit yourself. But we're not turning back if you get cold."

These characters unmask themselves and their relationship without appearing to tell each other what they should already know.

Vehicles for Conveying Exposition

Several techniques combine exposition with explosion.

Provocative Image: Dramatic moment.

> Two of my husbands on one park bench? When I divorced Steve three years ago, I left him only legally.

A showstopper like "two husbands on one park bench" can introduce vital information.

Monologue: Internal musing.

> How do I get into these situations? After three years I still feel like we're married. Unwilling to hurt Steve, I say, "Sure, I'll be at Jackson Square." Then I remember about Theodore. In five minutes my ex and present husbands get to do street music with me—and each other. New Orleans jazz won't be the best Blues.

You may want to justify a narrator mentioning facts, posing questions, or answering them. In the example above, perhaps the woman talks with someone on the bench beside her or writes her daughter a letter. In Ring Lardner's famous short story, "Haircut," readers find the monologue legitimate because a customer represents the audience. In theatre, audiences accept the convention of the aside, where a character leans forward to share private musings. In print, though, declaiming to an imaginary audience sometimes seems artificial. Devise a pretext for the monologue or make the tone captivating enough to foster suspension of disbelief.

Flashback: Return to the past.

> I sit in Jackson Square waiting for my husbands. Sunlight hits the street musician's trumpet with a flash golden as a wedding ring. Looking ahead, I see not the Square but the church where I married my first husband.
> Steve slips the ring onto my hand. Its gold reflects his eyes as he turns to kiss me, and I detect the glitter of tears.

Within credible flashbacks, readers experience no difficulty with tense inconsistency. Flashbacks seem familiar because any of us can await a green light or pause from wiping the kitchen table and effortlessly drift back to our first kiss, our best Thanksgiving, our last lie. You can capitalize on the familiarity of flashbacks, using them to link a character's past and present circumstances.

But by now some readers find the device over-used. Action occurring before your fiction begins lacks the immediacy of present conflict and can introduce backstory. Also, unless flashbacks connect seamlessly with the storyline, they distract from it.

The classic method of linking the flashback with the present involves sensual memories. In Marcel Proust's *The Remembrance of Things Past*, the particular flavor and texture of a *madeleine* (a French biscuit) dipped in herb tea conjure Swann's lost love. As he takes a bite, readers revisit his past with him. Authors can deliver such visitations in past or present tense.

Of course transitions and verb tenses always deserve attention, but flashbacks often require extra care. You can segue readers in and out with emotion (she remembers the last time she felt such anger), sensory experience (he hears his own boyish voice delivering Handel), dialogue ("On the beach?" She closes her eyes, seeing that stretch of sand), or object (as a boy he'd loved pink hair ribbons on girls). The section in this chapter on transition presents additional possibilities.

Perhaps you find the transitions associated with flashback less troubling than the verb tenses. You have more choices than you realize.

You can choose present tense for the body of the story and past tense for the flashback, or, after a good transition, past or possibly present tense for both sections. Relating the flashback in past tense communicates clearly but feels remote, while present tense provides immediacy yet sometimes causes confusion. Weigh your options. If you feel confident, experiment with tenses—whether or not you use flashbacks.

Theoretically, you can revisit the past via flashback more than once within a novel or even a short story. As usual, moderate. Immediacy must balance any remote excursions, and keep these in the background. A flashback that seems like a plot device hurls readers from your fictional world back to concern with a dental appointment, grocery list, or dessert.

SUPPLYING COMPLICATIONS

After establishing the obstacle or problem controlling your fictional world, you can trace character movement toward an intention or goal.

> Roger trudged out of the room as if he hoisted a heavy weight with each step.

Why? Why does he move like that?

What happens when Roger attempts to resolve his difficulty? If other characters oppose a character, then actions elicit comparable reactions, like equally matched teams in a tug of war. Roger quits his part-time job. What can happen? His business venture fails, and his wife leaves him, or—he and his wife throw a celebration party for their employees. At the gala, however, Roger rekindles his friendship with Caitlin, who offers an enticing business proposition.

Plot Thickening

A storyline that introduced Caitlin earlier sets up credible complications to follow. Without misleading, distracting, or giving everything away, how do you add the clues that tangle plot? Projecting at least ten possible outcomes from the initial conflict helps generate a coherent whole. You needn't write any of this down. Nor does imagining possibilities prevent your pursuing some route you discover later. But brainstorming familiarizes you with the scenario of your fiction and fosters an organic relationship between events and outcome. The more you speculate on plot eventualities, the better you do with whichever eventuality you select.

What can result from a protagonist leaving her cruel, unloving husband?

1. She becomes lonely.
2. He becomes lonely.
3. He kills himself.
4. She kills herself.
5. Their children do poorly in school.
6. Responding to lack of tension in the home, their children perform wonderfully in school.
7. His parents unequivocally refuse to forgive her.
8. Her parents unequivocally refuse to forgive him.
9. His parents unequivocally refuse to forgive him.
10. Her parents unequivocally refuse to forgive her.
11. She falls in love and lives happily ever after.
12. He falls in love and lives happily ever after.
13. She wins the lottery but won't share.
14. He wins the lottery but won't share.
15. She wins the lottery and shares.
16. He wins the lottery and shares.
17. He reforms, and she takes him back.
18. He reforms, yet she won't take him back.
19. He doesn't reform, and co-existing in the same small town seems impossible.
20. He doesn't reform, but she still takes him back.

A list can explore consequences emerging from a single conflict. Yet this list illustrates that brainstorming generates both valuable and ludicrous alternatives. The next step involves selecting one option, such as the last one, and exploring nine or ten possibilities for that.

20. He doesn't reform, but she still takes him back.

    1.) She accepts his flaws, and they live happily ever after.
    2.) He has an affair.
    3.) She has an affair.
    4.) Their oldest daughter confronts him about his cruelty.
    5.) Their oldest daughter confronts her about her passivity.
    6.) Their oldest son confronts him about his cruelty.
    7.) Their oldest son confronts her about her passivity.
    8.) Disgusted with his behavior, she leaves him again.
    9.) Disgusted with her behavior, he walks out.
  10.) Lonely, he falls into a deep depression.
  11.) Lonely, she falls into a deep depression.
  12.) They begin couples counseling, which proves successful.
  13.) They begin couples counseling, which proves unsuccessful.
  14.) They take a folkdance class and rekindle their former romance.
  15.) They take a folkdance class, and he meets someone there.
  16.) They take a folkdance class, and she meets someone there.
  17.) Their children encourage them to file for divorce.
  18.) Their children squabble over their filing for divorce.
  19.) Appalled, their children quit speaking to him.
  20.) Appalled, their children quit speaking to her.

Brainstorming consumes time and effort, which not all writers expend willingly. One April a writer I work with asked for help with his plot. When I suggested plot exploration as illustrated above, he refused. "A clever idea," he replied. "Boring though! I want to produce fiction, not lists." The following March this writer admitted abandoning his first novel. "I got stuck 100 pages in—without any way to fix things. This time I'll try some lists first."

Sometimes nothing can save that first novel. Nor do all writers benefit from brainstorming or printing plot possibilities. Yet the best time to explore plot occurs long before you feel vulnerable about a narrative's inertia. At that desperate point even irrelevant material looks tempting—anything to instigate action.

Some writers attack faltering plot by adding superfluous characters, details, and incidents. Planning counteracts this. A roadmap for your plot insures action, even if that action stems exclusively from emotions and not the battalions of the Civil War or the nuclear warheads of a hostile nation. Preplanning also lets you visualize how each section meshes with the next.

Of course, many avenues can familiarize you with your plot. In *The Art of Fiction*, John Gardner suggests identifying the climax and planning backward from there. For example, maybe as a turning point you select the eighth possibility from the first list: "Her parents unequivocally refuse to forgive him." This character has lost the people who secured his status and income. Which events led there? Perhaps he never wanted to marry her; or maybe her parents never wanted him to. In either case, on his own now, he learns that former clients no longer require his services.

Suddenly the conflict escalates beyond his relationship with his ex-wife or her parents to his livelihood. One day he confronts an empty bank account without stock to liquidate or clientele left to contact. Maybe he can still apologize, swear to reform, beg her parents to forgive him, mortgage his brokerage, cajole old clients, or toady up to new ones. After trying all that, he has no options left. Perhaps the piece ends here.

In fiction the climax and conclusion can occur simultaneously or separately. Does the above situation peak with the devastated protagonist contemplating suicide? Will he swear to join Alcoholics Anonymous and reform? The narrative concludes with members of the Horizon Bay Country Club voting to oust the man they once elected president. The last image captures the protagonist ruminating on past mistakes as he drives the car he must sell into the glaring sun. You can close with the main character fretting in his car or threatening his ex-wife or her parents. In all instances you benefit from envisioning the decisions or events resulting in the climax. Foreseeing an outcome doesn't mean you must use it!

CONCEPTUALIZING TRANSITIONS

When writers plan how one event connects with another, readers travel a fictional world more comfortably. Life prepares us to leap from moment to moment without benefit of logical connections. "Monday was great," we gloat. "Thursday? I didn't accomplish one thing." What links that super day with that crummy one? Neither life nor speech necessarily provides the transitions needed to join each scene, paragraph, or description with what follows. But fiction readers expect—and deserve—connections. Some writers mentally add transitions between sentences and paragraphs and fail to record these on paper. Other writers, turned off by abstractions like *later* and *but* or clichés (*meanwhile back at the ranch*) omit transitions on purpose. Still other writers underestimate the significance of smooth links, considering these trivial compared with vital characters and fast-paced action. Yet without transitions, how can readers follow characters from place to place?

Transitions operate both at the level of individual sentences and between the scenes and moments of the fictional world. Like an elegant piece of furniture, fiction needs graceful lines cemented by unobtrusive connections. Ideally, character and plot manufacture those unobtrusive connections through character feelings, sensations, and reaction to environment. Again, planning fosters artless transitions. If you visualize key moments in advance, you can evolve them in relation to each other.

Not all transitions wield equal power. Examples like *Quite unexpectedly, she found herself back in her apartment*, or *He woke, relieved it had only been a dream* can seem almost comic. These connections signal manipulation, coincidence, or formula. Provide clues that blend with the plot line.

1. *Dialogue*   "So, I'll see you at the restaurant."

    "I don't expect you to be late next time."

    "How do you like my new place?"

2. *Setting*   Mark hadn't turned on the lights in his apartment.

    The cabin never looked any different.

    Beaches at sunset provoke introspection.

3. *Emotion*   Sabrina was crying. Upstairs, David was pacing.

    Cleo bit her lip, as if that could undo the test results.

    Sam's anger hadn't subsided at all.

4.	*Weather*	Karen grimaced: the rain had changed to snow.

To blot out the wind's howl, Bob whispered the multiplication tables to himself.

Transfixed, Marcia watched storm clouds gather over the rented tables and chairs.

5.	*Image*	Flo sped down the Interstate, seeing not the cars but the diamond clips from the jeweler's case.

The last time Brett took out his wallet it still had five twenties inside.

Susan's muffins looked short and squat, nothing like those Pete devoured at Ann's brunch.

6.	*Symbol*	Shivering, Tom remembered his grandfather handing him the watch.

No matter where Nan moved, she still imagined that oak guarding her bedroom window.

Pat lifted the packet of letters. Yellow and brittle now, they'd lost none of their impact.

7.	*Time*	By noon when Dick called, Barb had already decided to decline.

"Haven't we done a lot for five weeks' work?"

"It isn't yesterday any more," the CEO reminded the chief engineer.

Transitions involving time attract the most attention, so seek other options. Disguise transitions. Exposure of essential underpinnings resembles a trace of white slip escaping the hem of an otherwise attractive black dress.

Like exposition, transitions often involve telling. When that judges or editorializes, it distances reader from character:

Kathy loathed Dr. Cyr's impatience with her occasional tardiness.

Distinguish such telling from the necessity of connecting one time or location with another:

> Kathy slammed the apartment door. Dr. Cyr should understand that if he didn't make her wear a dark blue uniform, she wouldn't need an extra ten minutes every morning to remove dog fur. She shed her coat while racing past his office. "Hi, Dr. Cyr," she called. "With you in a sec."

In some instances, telling conveys what you can waste awkward passages trying to show.

WRAPPING UP

Transitions have smoothly transported readers from initial explosion to final climax. Now it's time to conclude. *And, dear reader, they lived happily ever after* formerly ended numerous novels without engendering a single complaint. Today, though, certain people accept tidy resolutions, idyllic happiness, or flawless packaging mainly in satire. Of course, readers still expect fiction to provide order and mysteries to reveal who did it. But neither assumption requires resolving every detail.

For example, in Raymond Carver's short story, "Cathedral," the protagonist achieves an almost involuntary epiphany. By sheer accident he experiences the cathedral, the human monument to god, along with a blind man. Yet the main character expresses neither joy nor excitement. Readers themselves determine what this experience means. And many readers leave the short story wondering whether this insight permanently transforms the sighted man.

In life we ignore all sorts of opportunities; slip-ups and setbacks intervene. Change rarely comes freely or easily. So the fictional world either simulates reality or risks reader disbelief. Credibility suffers a similar blow with a sudden shift from greedy and callous to tender and caring, or, following one therapy session, from wallflower to life of the party. *I blinked. It was only a dream after all* obliterates originality. Instead, a climax foreshadowed in an understated way supplies a plausible yet surprising ending.

How do you tidy up without stretching credibility? Preserve the illusion of reality you introduced initially. Good endings often imply resolution. Ernest Hemingway's *The Old Man and the Sea* suggests that much has changed following the fisherman's great struggle; people often remember the novel ending this way. Yet the saga terminates with the old man dreaming as he did at the start.

This ending feels resolved, a result some writers like to plan in advance. Toni Morrison insists that "I always know the ending; that's where I start." (Winokur, 37) John Gardner, on the other hand, disputes the validity of knowing the ending in advance: "I think this is usually a bad idea, producing fiction that is subtly forced, or mechanical." (Gardner, 176) This contradiction confirms that more than one route leads to the words *the end.* Familiarity with your characters can assist whether you foresee an ending or let one evolve.

When character, plot, and outcome meld, the fictional world seems consistent. This can form the sort of finale that makes readers murmur *aha.* Superb endings make readers vocalize *aha* out loud. This potential exists if events lead credibly but unpredictably toward the conclusion. Determination to create perfection from disarray can produce improbable or oversimplified outcomes. Some victories bring scant happiness, just as many crimes remain unpunished. Guarded optimism seems more believable.

Nor should protagonists resolve conflict either through inexplicable coincidence or miraculous external forces, now called *the cavalry save.* Centuries ago, Aristotle labeled this technique *deus ex machina,* which in Latin literally means that the gods disembark from a supernatural apparatus to exert celestial powers that save the day.

Miracles, haste, or tedium can ruin the ending. Picture yourself savoring the last page of a good short story or novel. You wouldn't want the writer dashing through the best parts. Neither would you tolerate imprisonment in a relentless conclusion. Don't make your protagonist falter, rally as if to deliver an aria, sink into a faint, and revive to proclaim several more times before perishing (much to the relief of certain spectators). Who wants the audience questioning what took so long?

Nor should the audience wonder whether you have any beliefs, since your fiction disguises every one of them. Fiction has always revealed a moral code. Jane Austen argued against prejudice and pride, Mary Shelley against irresponsibility, William Thackeray against vanity, and Harriet Beecher Stowe against slavery.

Though today's readers seldom expect the ethical packaging once deemed compulsory, those same readers often applaud moral conclusions, albeit ambiguous ones. If fiction seems no more equitable or orderly than reality, has fiction retained its purpose? Ambiguous endings sometimes intrigue, yet many readers seek new insight. Realistic but fair conclusions turn folks on. Justice prevails; the greedy pay. Unless the harsh realities of the fictional world make success unimaginable, readers enjoy seeing hard workers and good guys win.

As Henry James put it, forceful fiction closes with "a distribution at the last of prizes, pensions, husbands, wives, babies, millions, appended paragraphs and cheerful remarks." (Lodge, 224) This advice still applies, though only if readers find the conclusion credible. Fiction must neither hang suspended nor screech abruptly to a halt. Think like a reader, and you hone your intuitive sense of what suggests closure.

Options for Ending

Open: Readers determine the meaning.

Gary's eyes turned away from her, out toward the sea.

Resolved: Unambiguous outcome.

Snatching up all she could carry, Evelyn rushed to the car. Al couldn't imagine trying to stop her.

Parallel to Beginning: Echo of initial situation or image.

The spires of the cathedral filled the landscape out Di's window ...

Even in the darkness, even with her eyes tight shut, Di still saw those cathedral spires.

Monologue: Character comments.

They're on their own now—to manage best they can. An old Collie like me can't take care of an entire neighborhood forever.

Dialogue: Characters converse.

"Your hair's getting silver."
Nance grinned. "Think yours isn't?"

Literal Image: Setting or aspect of setting resolves the plot.

> They predicted more rain, and the river had already risen more than eight inches.

Symbolic Image: Details represent a meaning beyond the literal one.

> Under a moon bright enough to read by, Ellie headed back to her cabin.

MAINTAINING INVISIBILITY

Conceal the stratagems that advance plot from initial explosion to final resolution. Don't distract readers with those hands moving levers and pressing buttons to stage the next event. You can learn more about disguising plot machinery by rereading your favorite fiction to notice how other writers keep readers involved instead of drained and exhausted. Initially, you may notice only what you like. But once you detect difficulties with pacing or credibility in other people's plots, you can find these in your own work.

STRETCHING EXERCISES

1. Explode into scene.

   Don't let yourself ease in by describing the setting and conveying the background. Introduce conflict in the first sentence.

2. Complicate the plot with a character's unwise decision.

   Have a character grasp at straws to reach a goal or escape a difficulty. What happens because of this?

3. Shift out of flashback.

   Provide a smooth transition from past to present. The popularity of flashback as a device to open novels has decreased. Yet the strategy still has merit.

LOOKING BACK, THEN AHEAD

Georgina began by letting her plots emerge as they occurred to her. The characters got to do anything they wanted. After several short stories that offered seventeen or eighteen characters answering the phone and walking the dog, she adopted a new approach. Georgina tried rigid plotting. She knew what the characters would be doing one hundred and seventy-five pages ahead. Any time she encountered an idea not included in her outline, she discarded it. Such material can endanger careful plans.

How fortunate! Many writers proceed most comfortably with a general idea of what's ahead. Yet they welcome continuous input from both their characters and their own inspirations. After all, in real life the most precise schedules rarely reflect reality. Fiction writers need at least that much leeway.

"Henry."

He sets down his coffee with a thud. "You don't give a guy much chance to study, do you?"

"Sorry. Ugh! You put milk in it!"

"Lots of people do. Don't look so horrified."

She tries to relax her jaw. The thought of milk makes her cringe. "Did you decide what you're going to do about Ashley?"

He examines his fingernails. "Nope. Haven't decided what I'm going to do."

"Just as I feared. I haven't decided what you're going to do either."

Georgina knows that Henry faces confrontations with the two women who make him most nervous: Ashley and his mother. But plans guarantee no more than a starting point. How do you get and keep your plot moving?

CHAPTER 5: Characters in Conflict

Reality in Action

To get your plot going, start a fight. (Georgina Raymond)

AMPLIFYING THE CHARACTER/PLOT CONNECTION

"Ashley. Good morning. Can I buy you breakfast?"

"Gorgeous day, isn't it?" Ashley yawns. "Wow, bet I'm late. See, I'm taking care of my neighbor's dog. He gets his pill at…" She leans over to check Georgina's watch. "…at ten minutes ago. Back in a jiff."

While waiting Georgina studies the piles of books, jars of shells, vases of feathers until Ashley returns. "Can I treat you to coffee?"

"Oh, no thanks. I don't drink it much."

"Anywhere you like then. Please let me do this. It's important."

Ashley smiles at something only she can see. "You know I want to help. I'm just not sure when …" She smiles again. "Tell you what. Tuesdays I buy groceries for the woman downstairs. Want to come with?"

"But, Ashley, I want to chat. We wouldn't even be able to …"

"Oh come on! Who knows what'll happen?"

Ashley will help determine what comes next and whether the plot is complex enough to maintain momentum. Georgina won't necessarily know that until she reaches the next event.

While developing your plot, focus on character and conflict rather than preserving any plan. You're better off letting characters and plot function as a mutually interactive open system. Character behavior shapes their growth or lack of it; this in turn affects their options. When you illustrate how each experience leads to subsequent motivations and events, you infuse your fiction with depth and sparkle.

Perhaps right now you'd settle for something simpler than depth and sparkle. Traditional plot formulas can help. Since antiquity, one scenario has involved a hero seeking a particular achievement, only to be foiled by a barrier or series of them. Today's heroes can battle internal demons along with dragons and armies. Obstacles can involve everything from crippling ambivalence, other people's expectations, or fate's cruelty—served up in contemporary fiction as bad luck.

If you keep elements like exposition and climax in mind, any situation can breed plot. You can illustrate a political position by tracing how a law or custom affects various characters. To expose economic injustice, begin with the death of a medical student's father. The intern panics about money. Does hardship make the student learn or change, or does your plot consist of scrounging for funds? The first scenario sounds like fiction, the second a nonfiction piece about money and education in America.

Avoid situations so didactic, simple, or familiar that readers feel like spectators dozing through a predetermined contest. Give your protagonist every valuable card and your antagonist a junk hand, and your fiction loses its power to reveal or influence. Like reality, compelling fiction assumes more charcoal shades than political commercials or warnings that *stealing buys only a guilty conscience*. If your fiction keeps drifting from initially complex dilemma to pat conclusion, try a new subject.

Emphasis on character in place of theme generates more believable and thus engaging plots. If your characters confront complex difficulties, those obstacles can stimulate change or growth. Any theme you include then emerges organically from the intersection between character and plot.

INSTIGATING CONFLICT

What initiates a plot capable of involving readers or illustrating theme? Make trouble. One character hates opera, especially Mozart. Jeff and Peggy disagree. Peggy calls Steve tasteless. Disruption alters either the internal or external status quo. Maybe for years Peggy has wanted to call Steve *tasteless*. Perhaps Jeff faces environmental change (a new upstairs tenant), addresses a chronic difficulty (a degrading job), or loses something either valuable or familiar (a relationship or a neighborhood bar). Such shifts generate tension between what characters have versus what they covet: security, sanity, or the sanctum of the golden past.

Conflicts experienced by multi-dimensional characters elicit greater identification and investment from readers. They already know all about boredom and want fictional experience to hurtle forward, wounding and healing in unexpected yet plausible ways. When characters lack options, readers predict what comes next. Tension disappears. Successful fictional conflicts keep readers wondering and worrying.

Checklist: Conflict

✓ Mystery

Explain just enough to tease readers. Never give everything away.

✓ Empowerment

Give both sides options.

✓ Progression

Keep intensifying the number and type of obstacles the protagonist faces.

✓ Causality

Hold fictional characters more accountable than real people. Characters who make mistakes frequently pay, and, at least in fiction, commendable folks often reap rewards.

✓ Surprise

Provide sufficient complexity to prevent readers predicting events too far in advance.

✓ Empathy

Encourage reader identification with characters and scenarios that pleasantly (or unpleasantly) resonate with their own sweet dreams (or night sweats).

✓   Insight

Reveal something about human nature.

✓   Universality

Present a struggle that most readers find meaningful, even if the details of that struggle reflect a unique place and time.

✓   High Stakes

Convince readers that the outcome matters because someone they care about could lose something precious. Trivial clashes often produce trivial fiction.

HEIGHTENING TENSION

Meaningful conflicts generate tension. Which factor sustains curiosity in every instance?

A toddler falls down a well.

A fisherman crashes through the ice.

During the decathlon, a heart attack drags a competitor to the ground.

Effective fiction exploits the tension that curiosity generates. On some level, so-and-so reminds me either of myself or someone I care about. This becomes serious. Will the so-and-so reminiscent of my deepest concerns survive? Prosper? Triumph?

Tension propels the art form called *fiction*. Some writers have experimented with disregarding this. Playwrights like Samuel Beckett tested works like *Waiting for Godot,* where the characters and audience sit around waiting and waiting and…Without suspense, however, drama and fiction ultimately disappoint. Suspense sustains involvement.

Tension functions comparably within a broad range of art forms. In the realm of music, tension involves:

1.   Foundation
2.   Postponement
3.   Release

The artist introduces an expectation (melody in music or conflict in fiction), teases this out, and unhurriedly resolves it. Regardless of your musical background, your fiction can reflect these three stages.

This progression parallels most natural functions, such as birthing, sneezing—even having sex. In that last instance, prolonging tension appeals because it titillates, at least temporarily. Fiction readers enjoy being teased while you divert their attention, while you postpone delivering the news that will lessen their concern. Yet teasing becomes torture if you interrupt to explain or describe. That can seem manipulative.

Sources of Tension

Tension needn't spring from behavior. Your characters' self-defeating or productive choices can keep readers involved. Still, internal conflict lacks a visible component. When do I tell my daughter that she's adopted? Make that struggle powerful enough to simulate action. Teetering on the verge of decision or response elevates tension. Consider Shakespeare's *Hamlet*. Genuine dilemmas, where both alternatives exert equal pull, absorb the audience as much as physical danger. Perhaps a wife wants to care for her aging father yet placate her husband, who despises her father's bigotry. When each possibility wounds someone she loves, how can this woman choose?

Like dilemma, irony also escalates tension. Two primary currents generate irony. In dramatic irony, readers possess crucial information unavailable to a character. For example, readers know that a husband intends to leave his wife, so they understand his responding with silence when she asks about next summer's vacation at the cottage.

A second strain of irony stems from a condition colloquially termed Murphy's Law: if something can go wrong, it will. A character's ill fortune can stem from the arrogance classically labeled *hubris*, or thumbing one's nose at the gods. Eric brags, "Well, I've got my promotion. Now we're set for life." Some unknown power soon punishes Eric's complacency; his wife leaves him, his employer goes bankrupt, or his daughter tests HIV positive. If readers care about Eric, tension arises from sympathy for his plight and concern for his future.

KEEPING YOUR READER BREATHLESS

Describing the present or future generates greatest tension. Often readers can't turn the pages fast enough when action arises from physical combined with psychological conflict, from interaction as well as rumination. Additional tension stems from withholding outcome while distracting readers with either secondary plot or delay. With this device the writer teases readers by withholding information about a source of great tension. Both strategies build suspense.

Subplots

All novels and many short stories need secondary conflicts, which must seem integral rather than tangential to the central plot. Sol Stein's excellent writing text, *Stein on Fiction,* suggests structuring the novel by interweaving distinct but interrelated plot threads. According to Stein, the first chapter introduces one conflict and ends with readers insatiably curious about that set of problems. In chapter two, a second conflict distracts readers. Just as tension mounts over that outcome, focus returns to the original conflict. The novel then alternates between the two plots until the final climax, thus maintaining—and heightening—tension throughout. (Stein, 103)

Stein presents this formula deftly but doesn't emphasize the urgency of maintaining coherence by closely linking those subplots. To illustrate, a husband can neither a) earn tenure nor b) tolerate his wife, who's already secured her niche at the university. Avoid irrelevant complications such as: c) a new zoning law threatens the couple's neighborhood, and d) their best friend suffers a nervous breakdown. Resist the temptation to insert unrelated material.

"Henry, don't you waaaant a weekend in Chicago?" Georgina detects the whine in her voice. She doesn't care.

"You know I do. I just don't want too much complication."

"How could your going to Chicago be too complicated!"

"You needn't shout. Would you look at me, please? Why gum things up with what doesn't belong?"

"But I want to..."

"C'mon, kiddo, you're not the only one who wants to. Remember me? I'm on your team. You don't get to add this excursion, though. Tell you what. Buy yourself a snazzy folder with waterfalls or kittens or something on the cover and store possibilities there. Then you won't ruin things because you want it all. Okay?"

She nods.

"Good. All fixed, right?"

Still staring at the floor, she nods.

"What's for lunch?" She pays no attention until he repeats the question at the top of his lungs.

Now she's ready to smile. "Leftovers."

Juggling subplots, even interconnected ones, requires skill and concentration. Too much complication irritates as much as too little. So do interruptions that seem contrived. Postponement, however, can create ...

Delay

Make readers wait to learn who survives a catastrophe. Provide new information about the characters (even as a toddler she dreamed about dying in a fire) or intensify the conflict (unless he proposes immediately, if they survive, she takes that out-of-state job offer). Skillful interruptions keep reader adrenaline pumping.

In contrast, illegitimate tactics introduce new subjects (the promiscuity of the protagonist's maiden aunt) before rejoining the characters trapped in a canoe during a tornado. Readers justifiably label this not prolonging suspense but cheating. Include only complications and interruptions that emerge from the central conflict. Hint at complications and interruptions in advance.

Elongate tension only so far. Just as with a rubber band, if you stretch beyond a certain point: snap, there's nothing left. Balanced plots combine descriptive passages with scenes that suggest immediacy by thrusting readers into the protagonist's conflict.

INCORPORATING SCENES

Scenes pump the blood in fiction's veins. Fictional scenes involve far more than scenery. In addition to physical location or setting, a scene offers a visceral enactment of characters in trouble. Either through verbal or physical struggle, scenes involve action. Consider the meaning of the term *scene* outside the realm of fiction. Parents often warn young children, "Don't you dare make a scene in the restaurant!" The subtext conveys, "Don't you dare cause conflict or tension. Attract no attention." As a fiction writer, however, you want your scenes to do exactly that.

Fiction reliant on authorial commentary or character monologue becomes static. Instead, provide dialogue, action, interaction, or combinations of these. Tension ebbs when only the writer or a single character verbalizes. Scenes, however, build on each other, reinforcing the sensation of a motion picture rather than a series of disjointed stills. Pause to recall your own feelings as a fiction reader. Like you, your readers seek direct interaction with the characters. No reader wants to hear the writer's voice filtering every experience through subjective perceptions and judgments.

Writers often underestimate the importance of scenes, perhaps because most writers generate summary more easily. Yet only scenes deposit readers within the borders of the fictional world. Perhaps Lucy mourns the loss of her neighbors—and their Golden Retriever, because her controlling husband forbids her adopting any pet. Interactions (or scenes) starring Lucy and her departing neighbors, their Retriever, and Lucy's husband reveal her plight better than commiserating passages can. Readers enter Lucy's world when they watch her husband's eyes remain on the televised football game as he repeats his refusal: *no pets!* Don't bar readers from the climactic moments. Scenes bring fiction to life.

Structure of Scenes

You can treat each scene like a self-contained fictional piece providing both initial explosion and final resolution. Begin with a bang and end with a bigger one at the opening and close of every scene. Accepting such responsibility arms you against rationalizations like, "Yeah, this scene drags at the start. That doesn't matter. After all, it gets so dramatic once she grabs the knife."

Regardless of how slowly scenes begin, true ones fling readers face to face with the struggle for some sort of power, whether emotional or physical. Every instance where characters confront each other calls for a scene. But never insert one simply because your fiction seems sluggish. Force yourself to question how each scene connects with what precedes and follows.

Checklist: Scene Components

✓ Clash between reasonably matched opponents or forces.
✓ Invisible exposition.
✓ Action, dialogue, or both.
✓ Location of characters in physical space.
✓ Concrete transmission of sight, taste, sound, smell, touch.
✓ Increase in tension.
✓ Irregular pacing.
✓ Seamless transitions.
✓ Intense emotion.
✓ Character revelation.
✓ Showing rather than telling.
✓ Immediacy.

MANIPULATING PACE

Scenes that feel tangible and charged with emotion involve readers in a race against time; they can't wait to learn what happens next. What do you notice when reading an effective scene? Surely it isn't Mikey and his mom getting their coats, finding the house key, and listening for the lock's click. What matters? Outside, Mom and Mikey, who just smashed Petey's bike, will soon share a small stretch of sidewalk with Petey and his furious parent. Such confrontations plunge readers into the action.

Balance between Scene and Summary

Sustained action exhausts. Both in stand-up comedy and fiction, timing is everything. Comedy flops when punch lines arrive too soon or late, when the audience detects mumbling or stuttering. Jokes also fail if the narrator runs out of breath. This pertains to fiction as well. Climax after climax becomes as tiresome as excessive description, lengthy explanation, or monotonous tempo. Balance between scene and summary also protects plausibility. Don't make readers wonder, "Can all that happen at once? The guy seems cursed." Having thought this, they lose the resonance between the character and themselves. Diffuse intensity with intervals when characters and readers enjoy a breather.

Teasing readers with subplots and delay heightens tension and establishes a pace neither static nor feverish. Cool readers down following torrid drama. In *Macbeth*, William Shakespeare gives the audience a break after King Duncan's murder. The drunken porter provides comic relief, or release from tension following intense drama or tragedy. The Fool serves the same purpose in *King Lear*.

Comic relief strengthens credibility. Like characterization, plot momentum must suggest reality—not reproduce it. Life fluctuates between humdrum periods and intense activity. Fiction, however, relies on the deception that events occur neither breathlessly nor tediously. Not every writer handles timing instinctively. Where do you need either more fireworks or more lake water lapping at the shore? Ironically, plot lacks internal rhythm: how readers experience events determines the sensation of pacing and flow. Sometimes, changing the order of events works wonders.

"Mr. Petry?" Georgina wants a supportive shoulder. "I wish someone would fiddle with all these confrontations, flashbacks, descriptions, monologues. If I took you to…"

He shakes his head. "Sorry, I don't know a single thing about …"

"I can't even count on you, can I?" Georgina feels sufficiently sorry for herself to turn on the TV and channel surf. Then, grinning, she clicks off the remote. "Look at this. If I move your argument with your wife from the middle of the scene to the beginning, I alter the pace without losing that lovely but slow-moving section! Oooh, Mr. Petry, I could hug you."

Henry's father rubs his hand over the thin hair remaining. Like one of Georgina's cats, he rears back.

ASSESSING PLOT STRUCTURE

Georgina now feels more confident about her plot because she's combined a little planning with a lot of flexibility. She stays alert. Good writers, like good motorists, anticipate bumps, construction, and unforeseen trouble. Readiness for the unexpected protects driver, pedestrian, writer, and reader.

Checklist: Plot

✓   Does the opening grab the reader's attention?
✓   Do you integrate exposition with storyline?
✓   Do you present a viable conflict?
✓   Do you provide a secondary conflict?
✓   Do you integrate all the conflicts you introduce?

✓ Does your fiction generate tension and balance its level?
✓ Do you intersperse summation with scene?
✓ Can readers participate in action and emotion along with the characters?
✓ Do you include necessary transitions and conceal their presence?
✓ Does your fiction move toward a climax?
✓ Does your ending either provide or suggest resolution?

STRETCHING EXERCISES

1. Integrate exposition with the storyline.

   Involve your readers while presenting the background information needed to clarify the character(s) and situation.

2. Design a secondary conflict.

   Introduce a problem or obstacle closely related to the primary one.

3. Invent three different outcomes for one scenario.

   Map out and resolve three different paths stemming from one conflict.

LOOKING BACK, THEN AHEAD

Georgina reads few thrillers, so she wouldn't attempt writing one. She's relieved that except in specialized genres, much contemporary fiction assigns minimal importance to overt action. Yet in all fiction, plot remains central because it involves the experiences, emotional or otherwise, of the characters. The movement toward resolving or failing to resolve a source of tension renders the fictional world both credible and captivating. Ideally, at least one character simulates a realistic, fleshed-out person or being. That character's fate then illustrates any point the writer wants to make. Character ability to achieve and learn conveys theme.

This system presents character, plot, and theme as inseparable. Fiction's power stems from the momentum generated by vital characters struggling to circumvent obstacles and achieve goals. Having set the stage with character, plot, and the potential to convey theme, you're ready to select the optimal perspective for recounting events.

Fiction writers often narrate in whichever point of view pours forth when they begin writing. But point of view controls reader perception of the fictional world. Perspective exerts too much power to justify a habitual or random approach.

Georgina started out writing everything in first person, the point of view she found easiest. Narrative poured forth, reminding her of the diary entries she penned as a kid. Of course first-person narrative needn't resemble an adolescent journal! Consider the magnitude of F. Scott Fitzgerald's *The Great Gatsby* or Ursula LeGuin's *The Left Hand of Darkness*. Neither first person nor any other point of view is optimal for all fiction. You wouldn't want to read only one point of view. Why write everything one way?

Sounds good, but where does it explain which point of view to use? The explanation surrounds you. Georgina now notices point of view in everything she reads, watches, and hears. To familiarize herself with the advantages and disadvantages of various perspectives, she plays with alternatives. What if Mrs. Petry conveyed Henry's adventures? Henry flinches. Georgina reminds him that it's only an experiment. How did Georgina move from experiment to selecting the point of view for her novel?

CHAPTER 6: Point Of View

Versions of Reality

Which is better: The first person narrative or the third person? Neither, in absolute terms. Some stories require the one, some the other. (Paul Horgan, 53)

CHOOSING POINT OF VIEW

"Henry, when did you first suspect that your mom didn't love your dad? I'd like to hear about it."

"Yeah?" He winks at her. "What do I get for answering?"

"Surely you're not hungry. You've had every course except dessert."

"And?"

She sighs. "It's like feeding a hummingbird, and you're not even real."

"That's why I eat so much."

Georgina signals the waiter for a menu. "Just give me my story."

Henry sets down the now empty breadbasket. "Your story? Don't remind me it's not mine. Some people have all the luck. Some people are smart, funny, confident ..."

"You're smart and funny."

"Why can't I choose my assets? I'll trade confident for clever any day. Then I wouldn't think twice about asking Ashley to ..." Studying the menu, he frowns. "If everyone gets to know all my problems, I'd as soon describe them myself." He flicks his lighter, a habit left over from his smoking days. "How 'bout I ask you a question?"

Georgina shrugs.

"If I gave my side, wouldn't that influence how people see me?"

"Of course. But we can't always have that. People discuss us behind our backs, make up stuff...Henry, you looking for an argument?"

"No, Georgie, honest. It's just...we have to take what we're dealt: where we're born, our parents—that stuff. So we like to defend our wins and losses, explain our actions. Sometimes you make me sound like a jerk. If I gave my side—took the witness box in my own defense—I'd seem, well, stronger. Starve me for a week; I'll still think that."

Henry's on the right track. Input from characters, readers, and writer creates a fictional world. Yet point of view, or the perspective chosen for delivering the narrative, exercises greatest control over reader interpretation of characters and events. Readers perceive the fictional world through that controlling lens as events unfold from the vantage point of a narrator who can either be one of the characters or an external voice recounting from a position of full or partial knowledge.

Point of view involves everything except dialogue (what characters say) and monologue (what characters think). Neither dialogue nor monologue affects point of view. A narrator recounts events and perceptions. (Waldo thinks Lola's a guttersnipe). This differs from a character's spoken words ("You're a guttersnipe," Waldo told Lola) or silent musings ("Lola's a guttersnipe," I thought, watching her work the room). Whether or not quotation marks or italics distinguish character speech and thought from the narrator delivery, the distinction between point of view versus dialogue/monologue pertains.

Point of view refers to the angle of perspective, which differs from viewpoint. In conversation people use these terms interchangeably. When describing fiction, however, point of view refers only to who narrates and how much access to information that narrator possesses. Fiction is delivered from a particular point of view and usually reflects a viewpoint, a general term for how someone sees the world. Writers reveal viewpoint through plot outcome, symbolism, or mouthpiece, an optional device involving a character presenting the author's viewpoint.

Viewpoint of character and author often differ. Consider *Moby Dick*, where Herman Melville exposes the results of Captain Ahab's thirst for vengeance. This character willingly risks the lives of his crew in order to annihilate the white whale. In contrast, from Melville's viewpoint the Captain's actions are irresponsible, even demented. By illustrating the consequences, fiction convinces readers of the validity (or invalidity!) of a particular viewpoint. Handling viewpoint perplexes few writers. Point of view, however, is another matter.

In *Moby Dick* or any other fictional work, various point of view options could confirm that Ahab is either justified or deranged. If the Captain recounted his story in first person (*I*), he could defend his attitude or expose his lunacy. The White Whale could deliver a first-person account offering a cetacean view of the Captain. Alternatively, a third person narrator (*he, she, it*) could relate the clash between Ahab and his enemy.

Perhaps this story belongs to Ahab regardless of who narrates. Yet point of view differs from who plays a starring role. Maybe you remember that Melville introduces a first person narrator ("Call me Ishmael"), who subjectively appraises Ahab. In the process Ishmael reveals the Captain, the rest of the crew, and himself. People can rightly argue that Ahab's vindictiveness makes him the larger-than-life protagonist of this novel. Yet Ishmael's perspective does more than bring us aboard to watch Ahab hurtle toward destruction—right along with Ishmael. Ishmael's perspective controls how readers perceive every character and event. Without that sailor filtering the narrative, our common vocabulary might not include the name *Ahab*.

Melville gave Georgina enough trouble in college. Unwilling to ponder the point of view of his novel further, she seeks Ashley at Releaf. Incense thick as tea leaves at the bottom of the cup sickens Georgina, but Ashley practically lives here. Georgina unclenches her teeth and enters. Through the haze, Georgina spots Ashley and calls her.

Ashley pats the cushionless bench. "Join me," she mouths across the noisy room.

Georgina plunges right in. "Hi. I wanted to ask you about Henry, because ..."

"I'm so glad to see you! And I want your opinion about the story I'm working on."

"Yes. But Henry ..."

"I've tried opening in first or third person. I can't decide which is better. Do you think ..." A woman implanted with three nose rings signals from behind the counter. "I'm so sorry, Georgina. I have to go. Can I get you some green tea?"

Morosely, Georgina nods.

DEFINING POINT OF VIEW OPTIONS

If Ashley considers who narrates so important, could this text investigate point of view before plot? Absolutely. That arrangement could be more expedient. The order of chapters often entails certain advantages and disadvantages. Your decision about point of view involves a similar trade off. Benefits and problems occur when you choose first or third person, speak through your protagonist or another character, and limit the amount of information conveyed or confide it all. Do you hope that if each point of view has drawbacks you can choose randomly? Actually, the limitations and benefits associated with each perspective demand greater care—not less. Of course, neither you nor Ashley can decide without comparing and contrasting possibilities.

Note: Picture point of view as divided into standard persons (first, second, third), as special circumstances within those categories (retrospective, limited, omniscient), and degree of factuality or otherwise (objective, subjective, unreliable). Point of view can be ambiguous and open to interpretation! To help you visualize these categories, special circumstances and factuality are listed under the main categories of first, second, and third.

First Person

This presents the plot from the perspective of *I*; the narrator may be the main character, a minor character, or an observer.

Retrospective: The *I* narrator recollects a past experience.

> I still remember that stage. I approached it gulping air I couldn't breathe. I was 17 then.

Unreliable: The *I* narrator either misunderstands or lacks all the necessary information about events.

> As my sister lumbers to the stage for her award, all eyes watch me. Her award doesn't bother me. I'm seated, of course, yet I know everyone can find me in the crowd. I smile, knowing the audience cares only about me. I bow my head to acknowledge their homage to someone glittering like the brightest star in the universe. I'm that star.

> I watched my sister rush to the stage for her award. I sensed she gloried in her achievement.

Objective: The *I* narrator only reports.

I watched her approach the stage, inhaling deeply as she moved.

Subjective: The *I* narrator comments and is directly involved, though not necessarily in the central conflict.

My sister trudged toward the stage. I could imagine her labored breathing. She looked fragile, flighty—a bird willing to snatch one seed before escaping.

Second Person

This presents the plot from the perspective of reader (*you*) as participant.

Objective: The *you* narrator only reports.

You mounted the steps. You inhaled deeply.

Subjective: The *you* narrator comments.

You never knew an auditorium could stretch so far. Surely everyone alive could hear your heart. Surely everyone knew what you'd done.

Third Person

This presents the plot from the perspective of a *he, she, or it* narrator.

Limited: The *he, she, or it* narrator represents the filter of one character's perceptions and feelings.

She moved toward the stage. If they knew, smiles would become smirks. She doubted they'd forgive her.

Omniscient: The *he, she, or it* narrator knows everything about every character.

She plodded toward the stage, imagining them discovering what she'd *borrowed*. Her heart thundered. Longing to hear applause for her own contribution, her sister watched.

Many watching her approach the stage assumed that this great honor stunned her. Her friends, though, knew something was wrong.

Objective: The *he, she, or it* narrator knows everything about every character yet only reports, offering no more opinions than a machine.

> Inhaling deeply, she approached the stage.

> Inhaling deeply, she approached the stage. This can't be happening to me, she thought.

The machine could be a camera recording behavior and conversation or a special device that also detects thoughts.

Subjective: The *he, she, or it* narrator knows everything about every character and comments on it.

> She headed for the stage as if walking in her sleep. The hushed room followed her slow progress. Her heartbeat pounded like a drum on the rain forest canopy. Fearing everyone could hear this, she wished she were anywhere else. Her sister fantasized accepting the award she herself deserved.

COMPARING OPTIONS

Which benefits and drawbacks characterize the various point of view possibilities available to you?

Second Person

Because few people consider this point of view, one could begin here. Following a narrator who assumes the perspective of the audience pays off with originality and immediacy. But disembodiment and slow pace offset these advantages.

> The cop let go your arms, and you rushed past the seething river to the shell of your house. You stood face to face with its remains. They told you that missing animals hadn't necessarily drowned; they could have swum to safety. They repeated this about the animals many times. Your dogs could have swum to safety.
>
> You repeated that sentence as you touched your ruined things. Your water-stained clothes and smashed dishes, what used to be your home. "I can't let you try those stairs, ma'am—not safe." You nodded. Your house threatened you. So you didn't get to know what remained. You'd brought Shep and Nana with you and lost them to the sirens, the boats, the shrieking people and children. Again, you repeated to yourself: your dogs could have swum to safety.

This perspective can seem sluggish ("You repeated that sentence as you touched your ruined things"). Yet second person places readers within the actual scene so that readers confront possibilities directly ("Your house threatened you"). Readers see and experience every motion and emotion right along with the protagonist/narrator ("Let go your arms, and you rushed"). The reader feels deeply involved because the protagonist's words invite that participation: "You'd brought Shep and Nana with you and lost them…"

Second person works best with short pieces or portions of longer ones. Attempt this perspective only if you ground your description firmly. Unless you locate your characters in a tangible environment, your second-person portrayal may omit the details readers need for clarity.

First Person

Clearly describing the environment can prove difficult with first person point of view as well. Still, less experienced fiction writers usually find this perspective easiest. In fact I've seen writers rule out first person because they consider it effortless and potentially sloppy. Some claim that a perspective similar to journal writing makes controlling narrative difficult. Other writers insist that this point of view cheats, since speaking through a character implicitly endorses some telling. Consider this first person portrayal:

> I hate how my parents treat me. Endless nagging about cleaning up my room, getting good grades, staying away from the wrong people. I mean, like what's the big deal? Like, do they remember anything they learned in high school? They're always on my case about small stuff. Isn't it all small stuff?

Technically, this monologue doesn't tell because the excerpt transmits the character's opinion rather than the author's. Yet summation, no matter who delivers it, engages readers less than dialogue or action; a scene would bring readers face to face with the conflict over "small stuff." Third person encourages such scenes. Like every point of view, however, first person provides distinct advantages. Skillful writers can intersperse commentary with scenes to reveal both the narrator and whichever character(s) the narrator describes.

Dollar for dollar, my folks spend more on us and our two kids than my sister and her four brats. So who do they love more, I ask you? Maybe I mean respect. They always push money at the factory worker. I get bashed at work and then my folks...Why, my snot sister shows up and my kids go nuts. "Hey, hey, there's Auntie Rose." Everybody knows it's just the presents. She gives pricey ones wrapped in silver foil with butterfly bows for Kimmy and dinosaurs for Tim. Rose's so blast-it competitive she guesses what Kimmy never knew she wanted. So she can't ask us first. Then Kimmy hugs old, thin-as-a-rail Rose who probably had liposection, or whatever. "Oh, Aunt Rose," Kimmy wails, "I love you." Some people don't get nothing from their own kids and have to suck up other people's. And they say our parents love me more.

In 154 words this narrator discloses much about himself, his sister, and their parents. Readers infer that the narrator is uneducated, or at least sounds that way ("liposection" and "don't get nothing"). He's jealous ("my snot sister," "suck up other people's") and suffers from poor self-image ("get bashed at work").

In contrast, his sister makes good deductions ("what Kimmy never knew she wanted") and prepares gifts elegantly ("butterfly bows"). As for the parents, what motivates them to bruise an already fragile ego by giving their son money? This point of view lets you develop several characters at once.

Kimmy's dad comments on the present. First person from a retrospective stance revisits the past filtered through the perspective of the present. This creates tension between the naïve child voice versus the more insightful adult.

I tucked the little jerks in, turned on the night-light, and headed for the kitchen. Mrs. Aln had urged, "Help yourself to anything you find, dear." Potato salad and brownies will help with skintight jeans. Sure they will. Of course she didn't urge me to try the cigarettes, dear. But nothing else interested me. I checked the sleeping monsters before I lit up. First I coughed so bad I thought they'd wake, start whining, and tattle later—ending my spending money for good. When I quit coughing, I exhaled and closed my eyes, picturing this trim girl.

I never mooched cigarettes again. A week later I was buying a pack a day. Food bored me; I could wear any jeans I wanted. And now, well, if nothing else, cancer's great for the hips.

First person retrospective often leads to telling, and incorporating scenes can prove challenging. But as works like Charles Dickens's *Great Expectations* and Harper Lee's *To Kill a Mockingbird* demonstrate, adult commentary on youthful experience can generate memorable narrative.

Whether describing present or past, first person unites narrator and reader through a series of secrets. The personal, confidential tone of first person subjective makes it the most intimate stance a writer can adopt. This particularly contributes to fiction involving dramatic irony, which involves readers possessing information that the protagonist lacks. First person can exploit the irony between reality and what the narrator fails to realize. In Charlotte Perkins Gilman's short story, "The Yellow Wallpaper," the narrator's husband confines her to bed, supposedly for rest and recuperation. While the narrator wonders whether lethargy will help her, readers discern that she needs not indolence but stimulation. The point of view emphasizes that this wife will escape the prison of her bed only by articulating the truths she can almost discern in the patterns of the wallpaper.

First person can thrust readers inside one character's blindness and perception. Yet the contrived device of an imaginary audience alienates some readers, as does the tendency to tell. Finally, this point of view can interfere with readers visualizing certain characters and empathizing with anyone besides the narrator.

Third Person Omniscient

This perspective incorporates the perceptions of every character, thus eliminating difficulty with describing the narrator's appearance or surroundings. Tension arises from contrasting diverse interpretations of truth. Since each character contributes to the overall picture, the point of view becomes a composite of every participant.

This passage illustrates omniscient subjective:

The handsome blonde adjusted the airplane pin on her lapel, always maintaining eye contact with the angry crowd railing at her across the fiberglass counter. Only that counter kept them from her throat. Naturally, during crisis they left her alone here. "I'm so sorry, ma'am," she told the next person in line, "there are no seats left. As I said earl ..."

"Do something for us, please!" They assume at 80 you no longer know that a plane holds more people than a shuttle, the senior mused. That blonde'll give the word, and the line becomes a pack of cheetahs after that bus. The hunched woman straightened, as if warding off attack. "If we knew how many spots…"

"No seats?" shrieked a man in an Armani jacket. "Can you airlines do something besides take money?" Eight people ahead of him, maybe seven, if he could shove past that little thing clasping her bag-lady parcel against her flat chest. He considered removing his jacket. "We pay top dollar for these flights, so you …"

"Please. Please!" The airline employee raised her arm to call for silence, then lowered it to wipe her forehead. She felt hot enough to pass out. If that guy started a fistfight those remaining could fit on one shuttle. "We're not responsible for fog, but we're doing our best to move you out. So please wait patiently for the next …"

The phone by her computer buzzed. She lifted it but heard only irate passengers. Enough already. "Would you please be quiet! Don't you care if I hear what they have to say?"

Third person omniscient subjective lets you zoom in on every character to reveal how they look and what they say or think. You can explore character thoughts without necessarily setting these off via quotation marks or italics.

The preceding passage contrasts several external and internal reactions:

The airline hostess:

"Only that counter kept them from her throat. Naturally, during crisis they left her alone here."

The elderly woman:

"They assume that at 80 you no longer know that a plane holds more people than a shuttle, the senior mused. That blond'll give the word, and the line becomes a pack of cheetahs after that bus."

Mr. Armani jacket:

"Eight people ahead of him, maybe seven, if he could shove past that little thing clasping her bag-lady parcel against her flat chest."

This point of view exposes the motivations underlying behavior. Such insight can deepen irony. For example, what if the senior's thinking concluded with, "Bet I could use my umbrella to pull a cheetah stunt myself"? Subjective omniscient provides the broadest scope and heightens tension by contrasting thoughts with speech and behavior.

However, sustaining this perspective demands great skill when introducing characters and shifting between them. Transitions become important. You must move smoothly between various characters and locations without telling about individual responses.

In contrast, objective omniscient confines the narrator to the visible signs that some sort of apparatus could detect. To convert the material above from subjective to objective would involve many omissions. The result could resemble this:

> A blonde adjusted the airplane pin on her lapel, while maintaining eye contact with the crowd railing at her across the fiberglass counter. "I'm so sorry, ma'am," she told the next person in line, "there are no seats left. As I said earl ..."
>
> "Do something for us, please!" The small, hunched woman straightened. "If we knew how many spots..."
>
> "No seats?" shouted the eighth man in line. "Can you airlines do something besides take money?" He fidgeted with his jacket. "We pay top dollar for these flights, so you ..."
>
> "Please. Please!" The airline employee raised her arm, then lowered it to wipe her forehead. "We're not responsible for fog, but we're doing our best to move you out. So please wait patiently for the next ..."
>
> The phone by her computer buzzed. She lifted it, then shouted, "Would you please be quiet! Don't you care if I hear what they have to say?"

This version lets readers draw their own conclusions about the scene captured by the machine's eye. Unless quotation marks or italics indicate that the characters themselves deliver their thoughts, an objective stance must omit character intention. In one sense, you heighten tension by thrusting readers into the scene. In this particular instance, however, significant detail is lost.

Nevertheless, omniscient objective proves effective in fiction like Shirley Jackson's "The Lottery." A neutral tone emphasizes the sickening discrepancy between character complacency and the horrifying death by stoning. Subjective commentary would soften the shock.

Regardless of subject matter, most writers find it challenging and not necessarily useful to sustain complete objectivity. Even Ernest Hemingway, the undisputed master of this technique, occasionally interjects subjective conclusions. Objective or subjective, omniscient point of view compares and contrasts the perceptions of several characters.

Third Person Limited

Instead of focus on many characters, third person limited offers the intimacy of one character's perceptions from the more distant third person stance. The contrast between closeness versus remoteness heightens tension. Readers follow one character. Yet because no first person voice is present, they experience the illusion of watching a film rather than reading a diary.

Note the effect of changing from omniscient to limited:

Shifting her weight off her cane, Mrs. Wilker looks from the ticket in her gloved hand to the tired blonde straightening the little airplane on her lapel. The flight attendant keeps eye contact, Mrs. Wilker notes. Why must she handle so much alone? The attendant loudly repeats what everyone already knows. "I'm so sorry, ma'am, there are no seats left. As I said earl ..."

"Do something for us, please!" Folks think at 80 a woman's too dumb to know a plane holds more people than a shuttle. Mrs. Wilker frowns. That blond'll give the word, and watch the line become cheetahs after prey. The senior straightens, as if fending off attack. "If we knew how many spots..."

"No seats?" shrieks a guy armed with a fancy-schmancy jacket and briefcase. "Can you airlines do something besides take money?" She can't believe people these days. Hotshot'd sell his grandmother for fifty cents; he'd surely knock her down to get in front.

"We pay top dollar for these flights, so you ..."

"Please. Please!" The blonde raises her arm to call for silence, then lowers it to wipe sweat from her forehead. She looks like she wants those guys to fight each other. Then there'll be plenty room for anyone still standing. "We're not responsible for fog, but we're doing our best to move you out. So please wait patiently for the next ..." Her phone buzzes. Guess she can't make out the instructions—an awful feeling—because she yells, "Would you please be quiet! Don't you care if I hear what they have to say?"

Which is worse, the senior wonders. Awful weather or awful people?

Does changing point of view change response to various characters?

In this version the narrator conveys the scene through the filter of one character's reactions. Since thoughts occur in present tense, that sometimes seems more natural than past would ("The flight attendant never loses eye contact with the angry passengers, Mrs. Wilker notes" versus "The flight attendant never lost eye contact with the angry passengers, Mrs. Wilker noted").

The perspective of a single character permits certain conclusions ("guess she can't make out the instructions") but not others ("only that counter kept them from her throat"). Although tempered by distance, third person limited can provide the same bond between reader and character as first person. In the illustration above, the narrator evokes not only sympathy ("folks think at 80 a woman's too dumb to know") but possibly some disapproval ("Which is worse, the senior wonders. Awful weather or awful people").

Of course Mrs. Wilker is one of many passengers condemned by fog. "Mr. Hotshot" could describe the delay so that readers feel either less sympathy for him or more. Third person limited tempers immediacy with objectivity, but the writer must deal with character absence from particular scenes.

SELECTING POINT OF VIEW

Every point of view involves both benefits and hazards. Sticking with one perspective helps you handle its problems. Once you lick transitions in omniscient, for example, maybe you feel reluctant to struggle with describing a first person narrator. You need courage to admit that protecting your comfort level doesn't necessarily enrich your fiction. That courage fosters experimentation. Even then, sometimes it takes many pages and drafts to determine the best point of view for each piece.

To escape that frustration, visualize how various perspectives enhance or limit characterization and plot. How does point of view affect key moments like the opening, the climax, and one or two pivotal scenes? Alas, such speculation provides no guarantees. Sometimes rewriting alone reveals what to do. But if you honestly listen to your fiction and not just your comfort level, you increase the odds of making a good choice early on.

At Releaf, Georgina's still waiting. Just as she decides that she can't take any more aromatherapy, Ashley slides onto the bench beside her. Georgina takes in the loving smile, the mane of curls framing Ashley's face. Sure hope this works out for Henry, Georgina decides.

Ashley offers Georgina a power bar, then smiles again. "You wanted to discuss point of view?"

"Why no, I want to talk about Henry."

"Henry?" So shy, so unwilling to get in anyone's way, Ashley thinks. She smiles down at the thin silver band on her right pinkie. "I've loved Henry for years."

"Then why don't you ..."

Three Nose Rings picks this moment to beckon Ashley again.

"Georgina, I'm so sorry! With Terri gone, I'm helping out. Wait for me if you want. Sorry that I can't promise ..."

Georgina attempts a smile, downs her tea, and starts through the incense. Listening to the blend of whispers and laughter, she tries to feels grateful. She hasn't connected with Ashley. But Ashley loves Henry—in one way or other. Besides, when Georgina switches from limited to omniscient she only has to cover four central characters instead of every voice in this hangout. Georgina closes the door on the sitar music and steps into the sunshine.

Relate your fiction from the perspective most suited to it. Point of view controls the information readers receive and the rate at which they receive it, thus shaping response to characters and events. The following versions of one scenario illustrate how much power point of view can exert.

First Person

Seems like everyone in this unbelievably big city knows each other. Maybe going to school in Denver was as big a mistake as mom warned. Hope Drama Club really wants new people, like that poster said. Imagine me trying out. What would my pals back in Mountain Village think?

Second Person

You wish you could shut doors, block openings, freeze time. Newcomers show up as if they own the place. Then those newcomers take all the good parts—and all the best guys.

Third Limited

Ann watches them drift in and out of her world. One month they have the lead, the next month they return to math, cramming for exams. Her world is Danny. Everyone and everything else relates to that.

Third Omniscient Objective

Sitting up front with other Masquers, Danny turns to grin at those entering. Kim, a tall blonde, chooses the first row. A heavy-set woman moves forward, glances at Kim, then settles down five rows back. Few men are present, and only Danny sits near the women.

Third Omniscient Subjective

Kim rivets Danny's attention. He stops talking to Ann mid sentence. Best thing I've seen in years, he decides. Kim tosses long blonde hair over her shoulder. From the corner of her eye, she checks the guy watching. Not bad. Still, there could be something better. Kim notices a fat girl in dowdy clothes sit down behind her. Kim's lip curls in disgust at the poor fat hick trying out. Of course they need someone for bit parts.

Point of view can propel plot and reveal character. In the following sketch, what is the point of view, and how does it contribute?

"Down Haven" — by Lisa Glueck

"I hate this place. Everything's so damn sterile. I belong at home and that's where I'm going to stay." Aunt Margaret turned her back on her niece and the Down Haven Administrator. *Why is Deborah always trying to tell me what to do? I'd shrivel up and die in this place. Just look what happened to Gertrude when they dumped her in one of these death traps.* She felt Deborah's hand touch her shoulder.

"Calm down, Aunt Margaret. Nobody's forcing you to move here right away. I just thought you might like to see the place and start to give it some thought." *She's the most stubborn person I've ever met. Three falls in the last year, and she thinks she can keep living on her own.* "We haven't finished the tour yet, have we, Mrs. Johnson?" Deborah looked at Mrs. Johnson and rolled her eyes.

Mrs. Johnson winked. "We haven't even seen the courtyard, Margaret. When the weather's good, our residents can take a stroll in the fresh air. We have our own little forest out here." Mrs. Johnson opened the glass door and led the way out into a small yard where several saplings surrounded a browning patch of crabgrass.

Margaret started to perspire. "Don't speak to me as if I were a child. I know what a forest looks like, and this sure as hell isn't one." *This woman is so patronizing, walking around in her high heels like the Queen of Sheba. Well, I was on this earth long before she was born, and I'll be damned if I'm going to let her shove me around.* Margaret turned from the courtyard and pushed hard on the glass door. It wouldn't budge.

"Hold on a minute there, Margaret." Mrs. Johnson took a key from her pocket and unlocked the door. "We certainly are in a hurry today, aren't we? I guess we're not a nature girl after all." *Oh boy, another behavior problem. We'll prescribe Valium right away for this one, or I'll go out of my mind.*

"Why did you lock the door when we came out here? Is this a home or a prison?" *God, this woman gets on my nerves; I don't trust her for a minute. She'll probably chain me to my bed once she gets me in her clutches.* Margaret elbowed her way past Mrs. Johnson and back into the yellow hallway.

"Don't be concerned, Margaret. We only lock the doors for the safety and security of our patrons. You'll have many opportunities to enter and exit freely here at Down Haven. You just need to ask one of the aides, and they'll be happy to assist you."

"Bull."

Mrs. Johnson took Margaret's arm and led her down the hallway, away from Mr. Fennimore. He banged his fists against the front door as he chanted, "Let me go home. I want to go home."

The writer remains invisible while this omniscient objective portrayal emphasizes how the needs of four characters conflict. All feelings and judgments are delivered through dialogue: "I hate this place" or monologue: "Why is Deborah always trying to tell me what to do"? Italics can distinguish what characters think from what they voice aloud. This format can prove especially useful with omniscient point of view, where you switch between several characters. Skillful use of character speech and thought lets Glueck show a clear yet understated theme. Deborah may have her aunt's best interests at heart, but Down Haven will rob Margaret of dignity and free will.

An alternative point of view, however, can prove equally effective.

"His Beard" — by Gail Sterkel

Sophie wasn't particularly attracted to that face, yet it kept coming back to her.

"I hate beards," Sophie remarked to Laura, Ann, and Marie. Sophie didn't like his beard—or any beards, which, she felt, left little skin for a friendly kiss on the cheek.

"Oh, I don't," said Laura. "I think it gives men a nautical look." Laura's blue striped top and white capri pants matched her thought.

"I think some men get tired of shaving every morning. They don't even think about how they'll look with a beard. It's a matter of—well, laziness, I guess," Marie told them.

"I don't think much about beards at all. I go for the total look, the whole picture." Ann used her arms in a graceful posture to emphasize the point.

"I just like their soft cheek against mine." Sophie felt her own cheek as she said this and shook her head. She always voiced opinions from dreamland, then shook herself back into reality. "Oh well. No matter. He doesn't think about me in that way anyway."

"Who?" they all wanted to know.

"Never mind. No one."

None had guessed that Sophie had anyone specific in mind. Now they were curious. "Tell us," and, "Yes, please do," coaxed a smile from Sophie.

"Hah! Sure had you girls going, didn't I?"

They knew she was lying. Each one planned to talk with her privately. Each wanted to be first to know and then tell the others. That's how it always was.

Omniscient subjective reveals characters and their conflicts as powerfully as the objective portrayal above. Limited third would obstruct the range of reactions. The point of view emphasizes the struggle over privacy versus curiosity and the competition between Laura, Ann, and Marie. Observations like "Sophie wasn't particularly attracted to that face," and "she always voiced opinions from dreamland" establish context and heighten tension. The subjective stance thrusts readers into a series of conflicts. Will Sophie get close to "that beard"? Can they make her confess "whose face keeps coming back to her"? Finally, who will be "first to know"? In this instance, objectivity would match neither the jocular tone nor the many conflicts.

Depending on the circumstances, first or third, objective or subjective may contribute more. The following list can help you choose.

Factors in Point of View Selection

Which point of view best helps you to:

- Start with a bang
- Deliver exposition
- Reveal character
- Convey character secrets
- Establish and sustain tension
- Balance pacing
- Describe with minimal intrusion
- Intensify the climax
- End with a bigger bang

COMBINING POINTS OF VIEW

Some writers solve the disadvantages of one perspective by discarding assumptions about consistency. One of the world's most famous stories contains one of the most famous point of view shifts. Jack London's "To Build a Fire" intimately involves readers in the protagonist's desperate attempts to survive deadly cold. But what happens after the protagonist dies? An omniscient rather than limited perspective would eliminate the need to switch point of view but also distance readers from the protagonist's struggle. London uses one pivotal sentence to move from the man's vantage point to that of the sole survivor: his dog.

You can label this point of view third person limited as delivered first from the man's perspective, then from his dog's. Or you can call this outlook omniscient, since readers follow two different perceptions. However you classify this point of view, the combination of two perspectives provides both immediacy and closure following death.

This is no easy feat, and few inexperienced writers tackle this challenge. Only flawless change of perspective fulfills expectations about point of view consistency. Moreover, within short works, more than one shift usually seems convoluted. Complex perspective works best in novels and can become elaborate. Both Michael Dorris's *A Yellow Raft in Blue Water* and Amy Tan's *The Joy Luck Club* combine a series of narratives in first person. In *China Men*, Maxine Hong Kingston combines myth and history with narrative delivered in either third or first person.

Multiple perspectives can seem nearly invisible. Rosellen Brown's *Before and After* alternates between first person and third limited. The father opposes the mother and daughter on handling the son's crime. Brown uses first person for the father's chapters and third for those from the outlook of mother or daughter. Interestingly, no chapters follow the perceptions of the youthful criminal. Readers may notice the absence of his perspective but often miss the shifts from first to third person.

Probably more readers detect intricate point of view in Wallace Stegner's *Angle of Repose*. Stegner chooses a historian for his first person narrator, interrupting his monologue with recollections from the narrator's grandmother, which are conveyed in third person. These lead to scenes, help shift between centuries and locations, and expose the narrator's subjectivity.

Point of view in Ken Kesey's *Sometimes a Great Notion* is more complex still. Kesey combines the perspectives of two brothers (first person Hank abruptly interspersed with third person limited Lee). Without break or assistance, Kesey adroitly leaps from one brother to the other's conflicting response. This apparent jumble of information captures the sensation of needing to process everyone's thoughts because one overhears them all. Despite unrivalled artistry, however, such experiments can overwhelm both reader and writer.

KEEPING POINT OF VIEW OUT OF SIGHT

Even if you never attempt such variations, you can gain much by noticing point of view in works like Brown's, Stegner's, and Kesey's. Familiarity with complicated combinations multiplies the options available for your own fiction. But keep point of view experiments out of sight. The most deeply immersed readers still notice a character conveying information she couldn't know, and readers who notice the narrator no longer inhabit your fictional world.

Checklist: Point Of View

✓ Have you assessed the impact of point of view on exposition, character revelation, and so on?

✓ Do you limit yourself to observations possible within that perspective?

✓ If you shift point of view, is this intentional and well disguised?

STRETCHING EXERCISES

1. Develop three first-person portrayals of one scene.

    Choose a family argument, a hospital waiting room, a crucial decision, or anything you wish. Each character should reflect both an idiosyncratic voice and a clear perspective on the situation. Compare and contrast three first-person versions of "truth."

2. Maintain objective omniscient point of view for at least one page.

    This is harder than it sounds. Even reporter-turned-fiction-writer Ernest Hemingway included judgments. You may never attempt an objective short story or novel, but this exercise exposes a natural tendency to judge rather than describe.

3. Change the point of view in one section of your fiction.

    How would third person limited alter material originally delivered in first person? What happens when you shift point of view? Experiment with changing a key moment or scene.

LOOKING BACK, THEN AHEAD

Georgina grins. Over cappuccino, she and Henry resolved their argument about who controls his story. He's a protagonist denied the added power of narration. Maybe she'll make him more confident as she switches point of view from third limited to omniscient.

To prevent further changes in perspective, Georgina vows to contemplate pivotal scenes and subplots in advance. Smiling, she stretches from the tips of her toes to the ends of her red hair. But at some point, Georgina—and every writer, including you—must integrate the separate components covered so far. This thought bolts Georgina upright from her relaxed sprawl across her bed. She moves to her window. Moonlight frosts her red hair.

Imagine Georgina's environment. What does she see out her window? Can you visualize her view or her writing space? You already know she spends lots of time on her bed (which must be large to accommodate the various cats). Scene after scene occurs there. Can you picture her dresser or closet? What happens to your relationship with Georgina if you see her flaming hair but not her bedroom, her window, or the moonlight sparking her imagination?

Another critical aspect of fiction remains. Even if your characters were born on Midsummer Eve and can float on air, readers must still see the solid land underneath those iridescent spirits. You must ground character and plot in real space and time. What happens to whom won't matter if no one knows where it transpires.

Georgina shuts her eyes to spy on Henry brushing his teeth. He grimaces at his reflection in the mirror. This time, though, she looks not at Henry but at his yellowish-green bathroom walls. How will Georgina integrate who Henry is with where he lives?

CHAPTER 7: Setting

Scenic Reality

When the conditions are right, live things creep up. The author does not need to airlift them in. No need to insert a reptile here, something symbolic over there. The most potent meaning arises indigenously. It looks like earth, like mud, like a log. The more your eyes discern the particulars of the physical world and its inhabitants, the more meaningful your work becomes. (Friedman, 92)

INTEGRATING SETTING WITH CHARACTER

Georgina squashes a spider darting up her lavender wall. Trying to wipe the dark smudge, she makes a larger dark smudge. Before she ruins the entire wall, she snaps her fingers at her protagonist. "Hey. Henry. Where did you grow up?"

"Georgina, I've mentioned that finger snapping before. You know perfectly well where I grew up. Why ask?"

"This isn't about moving from Brooklyn to Westchester. It's about the streets where you played as a boy. How big your room was. What you saw out your window…"

"Fascinating, I'm sure. But I can't remember a thing."

"Not even in exchange for what Ashley said about you?"

His expression changes. "What did …"

"Not so fast, Henry. Talk to me first."

He closes his eyes. "When we moved out of that dark little apartment in the city, I think our first house had a small backyard. Or, no, maybe not that one. Because I can picture…"

"This won't do." Intent on the details she wants, Georgina ignores Henry's offering. Leaning toward him, she can make out her neighbor's giant willow out the window. "I need to imagine that yard and you playing there. I don't care about the rest."

"News flash, Georgina. I'm grown up now."

"Doesn't matter. I want to see your toy trains, the color of your curtains...how it was when you were a kid."

"Too bad. I wasn't a happy one, so I don't remember much. I had thick glasses, and they called me ..."

"I know all that! I'm asking about your yard. And I know just who can help."

"Oh God."

"Mrs. Peeetrry, oh pleeaase give me a moment, if you would."

Georgina and Henry observe the reflection of Henry's mother observing her reflection in the spotless mirror above her Danish teak dresser. She checks the Italian rose marble clock, smiles vaguely at her son, and nods at Georgina. "I haven't much time. Before this morning's beauty appointment, I'd planned to get roses for poor Ethie Hendrickson. What is it now?"

"The apartment where you lived when Henry was born? I'd be so grateful to know ..."

"Henry was such a promising baby." She eyes the antique clock again. "You may have two minutes of my time." Mrs. Petry removes her Gucci purse from the brass umbrella stand, crosses the ivory wall-to-wall carpet, and sinks onto a ruby velvet Victorian loveseat. "That apartment was unfit for human habitation. Our Henry sat in that tiny yard by himself, and I ..."

The contrast between where Henry grew up and Mrs. Petry's present drawing room reveals much about this character. Georgina isn't finished exploring their habitat. After all, setting controls character development, thus impacting your fictional world as powerfully as your choices about people, plot, and point of view.

Consider some memorable fictional portraits. What would Atticus Finch be without the live oaks of Harper Lee's *To Kill a Mockingbird*? Can you isolate Hester Prynne from the Puritan community in Nathaniel Hawthorne's *The Scarlet Letter*? Take Captain Ahab. Can he hunt a rhinoceros? Even if you haven't read these books for years, you can probably still visualize the setting surrounding these characters as readily as the characters themselves. These authors left us landscapes along with characters.

Characters make those landscapes memorable. Unless we've visited places ourselves, we remember locale in connection with people. Well-developed characters seem inseparable from their surroundings. After all, doesn't environment shape behavior and personality? To intuit that inseparable connection, readers need a visceral sense of the landscape the characters inhabit.

PRESERVING BALANCE

Characterization, plot, and setting must work in unison. Yet some writers disconnect habitat from storyline, almost like moving a backdrop on or off the stage. Perhaps this division stems from the way some teachers approach literature. At some point, many of us learned to write about the main character, then the climax, and, finally, a paragraph each on setting, symbolism, and theme. Possibly such analysis helps introduce the elements of fiction. Yet dissection like this misrepresents the interconnectedness of fictional elements. Then, fiction writers tend to compose either description peripheral to characterization or characters that exist in a vacuum.

Setting moves readers most when it contributes to an organic whole. So close your eyes and picture your characters within desert, jungle, or suburb—whichever setting shaped them. Imagining this helps balance location and characterization. Right from the start, view your characters inhabiting a distinct place. Environmental detail added after you complete everything else can resemble a stage set for someone else's characters.

Characters must match their environment. Consider that relationship in classic examples like Thomas Hardy's *Return of the Native*. Some critics label Egdon Heath not background but part of the cast. This bond between character and setting pertains to contemporary fiction as well. To mention just one example, the ambiguous heroism of Oskar Schindler in Thomas Keneally's *Schindler's List* could never exist without the Nazi terrorism of 1938 Krakow.

If you mesh character with setting, your readers won't skim or even skip passages describing the scenery. Nor need readers interrupt your fictional world to scratch their heads and ponder, just where are these people having this conversation? Ironically, though, the readers who would notice the absence of setting never want to notice that the details in certain passages concentrate exclusively on scenery.

EXAMINING THE HISTORICAL ROLE OF SETTING

Contemporary readers require fewer details because fiction's role as dispenser of information has changed. Gradually, CD-ROM encyclopedias or Internet services replace the weighty volumes that once satisfied curious appetites. Graphic depictions have become as accessible as information. This has changed what readers seek.

To familiarize yourself with your readers' needs, close your eyes and picture a world without television and the formerly inconceivable media advancements now commonplace. Transport yourself back to when most people found travel difficult and expensive. Keep your eyes closed and imagine your curiosity about the world you've never seen: the caves of India, the deserts of Africa, even the ocean beyond reach at the other end of your own country. You've never visited these places and have seen only blurry photographs, and before 1839, no photographs at all.

You begin to realize what setting formerly gave fiction, so you can open your eyes. Lush, meticulous description constituted the average reader's sole access to places as exotic as Mars once seemed. Hungry to experience new worlds, readers relished the exact details often deemed excruciating today.

To confirm this, examine the openings of several great 19th and early twentieth century novels where setting plays a major role. Before Josef Conrad's narrator introduces any people, *Heart of Darkness* (1899) furnishes two paragraphs describing the Thames, the windless air, and the tide. Stormy sea and lonely landscape constitute the only action for the first four pages of O. E. Rölvaag's *The Boat of Longing* (1921). E. M. Forster's *A Passage to India* (1924) offers intriguing conflicts and memorable characters. Yet Forster devotes the entire opening chapter to the Marabar Caves, the bazaars, the Ganges, the temples, and the sky before any of those memorable characters appear.

Exceptions exist of course. In *Great Expectations* (1860) Charles Dickens describes Pip's history before describing the marsh. Within that setting Pip encounters dreadful danger two sentences after Dickens sets the scene. Even so, once upon a time, when the world seemed so much larger, few readers minded a leisurely saunter through marsh or cave or harbor before anything happened. Yet even with prose as exquisite as Conrad's or Forster's, some readers now grow impatient with motionless, people-less portraits.

Most readers want setting to serve character and story. Consider some of the many contemporary novels dependent on a singular setting. Dorothy Allison's *Bastard out of Carolina* (1992) could occur only in Greenville County, South Carolina, because environment constrains every one of these characters. Yet the first page never mentions setting.

San Piedro Island exerts similar control on the inhabitants in David Guterson's *Snow Falling on Cedars* (1995). Isolation constrains Guterson's characters as much as the sea restrains Herman Melville's Ishmael. Yet Guterson begins with a courtroom scene exploring the background of the defendant and the victim. Details about the heavy snow and the island's turbulent history follow introduction of the central conflict. This strategy integrates character with location. Today, setting contributes by reinforcing characterization and conflict.

FLESHING OUT SETTING

Though setting now supports rather than stars, fiction always needs a sense of place. Readers expect faster pacing while experiencing the physical environment with several different senses. Surroundings impinge on numerous aspects of character lives. Consider how setting has affected your own life, because this helps you analyze how environment shaped your characters.

Context

Realistic characters emerge from the fabric of their worlds instead of being sewn on top like sequins embroidering a dress. Understanding the character's world involves everything from date, historical context, longitude, and latitude to the number of closets in apartments or pizzas in freezers. But like the details and possibilities you store for characterization and plot, you—and your reader—benefit from your knowing more about setting than your fiction furnishes.

Integrate those details, or readers may wonder where the character went and start speeding through your pages to rediscover the vanished conflict. As someone reading like a writer, how would this description of a harbor strike you?

> The pungent yet welcoming sea-salt spray predominated, washing everything with the last glitter of the dying sun, now mostly done with its journey beneath the waves. Anchored boats with witty names embellishing their gleaming sides rested—waiting and rocking. The boats moved slightly, with no hint of impatience, as if everything

important lay ahead in a universe where time made no difference. The boats swayed on waves blue as eyes. The wind whispered. The mastheads clinked, clinked in the breeze. Light, not time, owned everything here. Salt smell laced the air, slowly and insidiously eating away at the anchored vessels.

Ribbons of iridescent light stretched across the late afternoon ocean—priceless jewels setting off the starched white sails and gleaming varnish of yachts harbored in the cradle, the very lap, of blue-green luxury. Silver and pearl bracelets of wave decorated the shore. Foam glistened with a hint of gold. Despite apparent motionlessness, nothing stayed completely still. Gulls circled, raucous with anger that in so much wealth they received nothing. Smaller birds tried to keep up, to grasp anything the gulls failed to snatch and cart off to a safe haven.

The sky hung suspended like a giant, unblemished sapphire promising power and potential. The gentle breeze cascaded light and shadow over that expanse of topaz, aquamarine, precious and semi-precious stone, seeming to bless it. On this late September day the amber light would not linger, would soon begin to fade into something else, as so many things must.

He walked swiftly, eyes straight ahead, anxious to get there before anything else happened.

Note how many more questions this passage raises than answers. The foreshadowing hints at wealth and loss but provides few clues about the characters or their struggles. Lengthy description overshadows the human inhabitants for three paragraphs; information that belongs in the background crowds the foreground.

At last a character appears, yet he seems disconnected from the preceding details. He's rushing somewhere. How does that connect with the harbor, the sky, and all those jewels and gulls? Does this opening create a fictional world or tempt the reader to continue? The details conjure a variety of senses—a fundamental accomplishment. Does that matter if the setting seems detached from the character? Wouldn't you call this description for its own sake?

Consider another version.

The pungent yet welcoming sea-salt spray washed everything with the last glitter of the dying sun. Everything dies, he thought. Shaking off this morbid reaction, he smiled at the witty names of the anchored boats. They seemed to shift almost imperceptibly, without impatience. Time doesn't always matter, he reminded himself.

The boats swayed on the blue waves; the wind whispered; the mastheads clinked in the breeze. Salt smell laced the air, insidiously eating away at the anchored vessels. Streamers of light stretched across the late afternoon ocean—setting off the starched white sails and gleaming varnish of yachts harbored in the cradle of blue-green luxury. Silver and pearl bracelets of wave decorated the shore. Foam glistened with a hint of gold. Nothing stood completely still. Gulls circled, raucous with anger that in so much wealth they received nothing. Smaller birds tried to keep up, to grasp anything the gulls failed to cart off to safety.

Light and shadow cascaded over that expanse of topaz, aquamarine, precious and semi-precious stone. On this late September day the amber light would not last. He sighed. Before long everything fades into something else. He walked swiftly, eyes straight ahead, anxious to get there before anything else happened.

This passage contains 203 words versus the 262 of the preceding. The setting remains vivid, suggests symbolic overtones, and incorporates sound, smell, and touch along with sight. But this version blends the scenery with the character's responses.

The second rendition also omits some of the heavy-handed language, like "waves blue as eyes," "the sky hung suspended like a giant, unblemished sapphire," and "as if everything important lay ahead in a universe where time made no difference." Description of setting sometimes elicits self-indulgence, and whether painting landscape or living room, writers can lose control. Several pages later they're still depicting the hill remembered from childhood sledding, the Egyptian mummies explored in the Smithsonian, or the Hawaiian volcano visited on last year's vacation.

Relevance

Unfamiliar subjects or locations also seduce writers into embellishing with irrelevant detail. Perhaps you fantasize writing a novel about geologists exploring Darwin's forgotten world. Having never been there, you research the Galapagos Islands. In your zeal you want to share every detail about those marine iguanas or blue-footed boobies winging above geyser and cactus. Fiction mustn't imitate an encyclopedia. If you long to devote page after page to lizards and birds, try nonfiction.

Awareness of excessive description helps counteract it. Describe setting like any other background detail. No fictional world can survive either endless trivialities or yawns over characters arguing in rooms that could exist anywhere and thus exist nowhere.

STIMULATING READER IMAGINATION

Readers who receive enough details to combine your images with their own imaginations enter your fictional world more actively. This sketch demonstrates how precise details can transport readers from a mundane grocery to a luxurious villa.

"From Meat and Potatoes to Caviar" — by Yenna Phillips

I was pushing my cart down the supermarket aisle, thinking of the dreariness of our meals. How bored my family must be. Searching for something to liven up dinner, I spotted a tiny can of expensive caviar. Lumpfish caviar. Lumpfish?

We were standing on the dock at Babol Sar on a sunny Iranian morning, awaiting the arrival of a government launch. Across the Caspian Sea, snow sparkled on the peaks of the Elberz Mountains. Smoke from cooking fires rose from huts dotting the tea plantations on the mountain slopes. We smelled coffee roasting in the village of Babol nearby.

Rainbows danced in the spray as our launch cut through the deep, cold waters of the Caspian. At the Shah's fisheries on an island twenty-five miles from shore, the Manager greeted us and led us on a tour. We had not realized how hungry we were until we emerged into the sunshine and heard our host announce, "Time to eat."

We crossed the green lawns set among fragrant eucalyptus trees. At the villa the mullah's call to prayer from the nearby mosque reverberated through the clear Iranian air. Servants in white robes and turbans escorted us through airy, high-ceilinged rooms to a dining porch and a flower-decorated table with snow-white napery.

On the table servants placed large bowls. I stared in astonishment at the contents—CAVIAR, beluga roe caviar, only the world's best, harvested from sturgeon caught hours before. I savored home-baked bread, newly churned butter, and tropical fruits including guava and pomegranates, served with a Persian wine and the BOWLS OF CAVIAR.

Afterwards, as I sipped from a cup of aromatic Turkish coffee, I felt a tap on my shoulder. A clerk in the supermarket inquired, "Lady, you seem in a trance. You all right?"

Uncertainly, I looked about. "Oh, yes. Thank you kindly, sir. I was just trying to think what to have for dinner." I tossed a can of tuna into my cart and hastened through the crowd of Wednesday shoppers.

With the thud of that can, readers return to the supermarket.

The writer needs no detail beyond "dreariness" to capture the first scene in this piece. In fact the initial absence of detail heightens the feast that follows. Every sense is awakened through the smell of the coffee, the sight of the rainbow, the warmth of the sun, the call of the mullah, and, of course, the taste of that caviar. The elegant setting and the mouth-watering food are not ends in themselves but vehicles for developing the worlds, both past and present, of this character's experience.

SUGGESTING VERISIMILITUDE

Just as your character's words should suggest rather than duplicate conversation, your setting benefits from simulating reality—not reproducing it. Substitute evocative details for information about climate, crime rate, or distance from the dwelling next door. The illusion of realism lets readers experience an environment. All that matters is the bloodstain, not the number of steps to the garage or condition of the carpet covering them. Must you reconstruct those steps? Describe a setting that either appeals to—or turns off—all your reader's senses.

To describe effectively, you need emotional distance from the places you remember or love. Ernest Hemingway warned,

> Never write about a place until you've been away from it, because it gives you perspective. Immediately after you've seen something you can give a photographic description of it and make it accurate. That's good practice, but it isn't creative writing. (Winokur, 8)

But don't rewrite the reality that readers know. For example, anyone familiar with the location of New York City's Plaza Hotel will sit up and take the wrong kind of notice if you plant that institution near the Statue of Liberty instead of Rockefeller Center. Double-check accuracy to avoid inadvertently dismantling the laws of place, time, physics, or biology.

LETTING READERS PARTICIPATE

Within the context of those laws, you can suggest location without delineating every feature, as the following sketch illustrates.

"Lefty" — by Marv Beatty

"Your roper's extremely skillful, isn't he?"

"Sure is, lady. Ol Lefty ain't missed but once this mornin'. I'd miss more'n half if I was roping calves and tryin' to read brands amongst all that bellerin'."

"Open the gate a little, Joe. He's draggin' out another. That's gonna be a big sucker to flank and throw down so's we can cut 'im 'n brand 'im 'n squirt 'im full of vaccine. Stand back a little, lady, so you don't get splattered. Green would look real bad on them white slacks."

"You're so skillful. I'm amazed at how fast you laid that calf down and did all those things to it. And that uh, Lefty kept the rope pulled just right, didn't he? Tell me, why does he turn his whole body and not just his head when he looks to the side?"

"Well lady, it's this way. Ol Lefty he lives by hisself way up on the head o' Trail Crick 'n raises broncs. Breaks um and sells um. Hell, his cabin's a good ten miles up the crick from his nearest neighbor. Well, three, four years ago one of them broncs bucked old Lefty off, 'n he landed on his head 'n broke his neck."

"Oh my! I hope someone found him right away."

"Nope. Three weeks or so before anybody knew. Lefty crawled to his cabin, splinted up his neck best he could, and lived off canned beans 'n condensed milk till his neck got to where he could drive down the canyon to the Bagley place 'n ask um to drive him to Miles City for a doc. The doc took a bunch of them X-ray pitchers 'n sed that if he warn't a tough old buzzard he wouldn't be alive. But there warn't nothin' could be done now that his neck had reset. That's why Lefty cain't turn his head. Don't hurt his ropin' much, though. He's breakin' his broncs just like before."

"That's unbelievable. Do you suppose I might speak with him?"

"Sure, lady. We're ready fer a break 'n some coffee anyhow. Slim, throw an egg in that coffee to settle the grounds. It's boilin' pretty hard. This lady won't wanta hafta chew it."

"Mr. Lefty, could I ask you a question or two?"

"Of course. I'd be delighted to speak with you. My name is Lamphere Chatterton, but please call me Lefty. Everyone else does."

"Mr. Chatterton, I mean Lefty, George told me a little about you while you were dragging calves out to be branded and those other horrible things. Have you always raised horses?"

"No, I was born and raised in Chicago. My family was in theatre there. After I graduated from Northwestern with a Masters in zoology, I started on my Ph.D. in paleontology at Yale. The first summer we did fieldwork, digging for dinosaurs about fifty miles north of here, along the Missouri. I fell in love with this country and vowed to return. After the second summer of fieldwork, I arranged for a job on a ranch. I thought it would be for a year or so. One thing led to another, and I'm still here."

"Is raising horses all you do?"

"No. The last ten summers, while my horses are on the range I've been excavating a Tyrannosaurus Rex skeleton that I found on my ranch. Next month *Science* will publish my paper on it. And the Field Museum has just purchased the skeleton. They paid more for it than the appraised value of my entire ranch with all my horses. So this fall I may hire a man to feed them while I go to Florida for a few weeks. I get rheumatism in my neck when the weather falls below zero. By the way, I hope you'll join us for some Rocky Mountain Oysters after we're done working these calves. Everybody around here says I sauté them just right."

The piece interweaves setting with plot. Only in the context of Lefty's accident do readers care where he lives, the distance from his nearest neighbor, or that a canyon separates him from Miles City and the doctor.

The irony of this piece underscores the danger of assumptions. Because Lamphere ropes calves on a ranch, the lady in the white slacks, probably along with many readers, draws various conclusions. The lady infers that Lefty always lived out West and presumes that he's uneducated, lacks skills outside the corral, and eats only beef, beans, and coffee you can slice. The dialect, the cuisine, and even the dinosaur bones cleverly capture one character's misconceptions. The setting, however, adds a whole other level.

ESTABLISHING ATMOSPHERE

In the sketch above, a few details about calf and canyon suggest all readers need. Today's writers often integrate setting and atmosphere with character and conflict. Atmosphere can arise from character response to surroundings, and understatement often conveys most.

Brief, oblique references to dangerous fog, torrid heat, or ominous darkness now replace heavy-handed attempts to create mood.

Consider how background music has changed in suspense films from the 1940's, the 1960's, and last week. Subtlety often replaces the dark chords, loud crescendos, and artificial sound effects that once foreshadowed disaster. Today's film or fiction audiences value emotional environment or mood yet expect innuendo. Details about setting can solidify atmosphere, from the sunlight on the sugar cane fields to the metallic impersonality of the skyscrapers. Plot can also establish mood: they'd warned her about being in the building alone. But how else could she finish the report? Ideally, atmosphere isn't a component to add but an impression evolving from the other elements of your fiction.

USING SYMBOL

Discretion becomes still more important when introducing a symbolic setting. The swing in the backyard can represent a child trying to glide past a depressing and dangerous environment. An unsentimental coupling of literal with symbolic meaning can move readers. Yet readers become uneasy once the swing transports the child over the rainbow lighting the ghetto, upward to the fairies offering rescue from squalor and violence. Readers become uneasier still if the child swings higher and higher, eventually crashing into a conveniently placed tree. Overpowering symbolism becomes uninteresting, because it shrieks (rather than whispers) the improbability of escape.

Also exercise caution with symbolism related to weather and climate. Such symbolism resembles a nineteenth-century device that can now seem heavy-handed. The literary convention of pathetic fallacy compares some aspect of nature (landscape, foliage, or animal) with a human individual. External surroundings manifest the character's internal emotions. The protagonist weeps, and rain flows from the skies. A youth sets out to explore the world while an adolescent bear leaves behind the comfortable familiarity of mother, den, and siblings.

In certain genres, such as Gothic fiction, readers often enjoy such comparisons. But in mainstream fiction, pathetic fallacy works best when such references never distract readers. Pathetic fallacy and other metaphors have lost power through overstatement or overuse that robs imagery of its original impact. The expression *red as brick* once evoked rust-red blocks resplendent under sunlight. Now, though, most readers skim this phrase without picturing anything. Choose either literal or figurative description that evokes tangible physical sensation. How could you describe bricks so that readers once again picture their color and feel their solidity?

Links

Accomplish this by complementing the familiar with something new: over the years, Eloise and her stepmother had dismantled the wall between them brick by brick. Or link the familiar with the fantastic: glancing away from the space station's *cryosite* panels, Jason remembered the red brick houses and white picket fences of his boyhood. Ideally, at least one tangible detail reverberates with universal images and experiences. Take that fence, for example. Not all of us grew up with "white picket fences." Yet we can still identify with the image of a fence: those we saw in the countryside, surrounding our yard, or barring us from the yards of others.

A fence provides a concrete image. You may decide to identify the fence or let your readers' imaginations design their own. Specific or generic, however, a fence replaces the abstract with the physical. Readers experience the moldy smell of old wood or the sound of chain link clacking in the wind. A sad, lonely place becomes *Ellen could hardly see well enough to move without crashing against the rusted farm machinery.* Involve as many of the senses (sight, sound, taste, touch, and smell) as possible. Rely on sight no more than necessary. Many writers lean on visual images, so a number of those have lost their power. Exclusive emphasis on sight also interferes with the illusion of reality. Most people encounter the world with five senses, although too few of us write that way.

Figurative details can enrich description. But use such language sparingly. Too many non-literal images—especially compelling ones—distract from the storyline and become less effective than too few. Development of a single symbol helps readers focus. If you start by comparing loneliness to a janitor mopping a mall at dawn, elaborate on variations of that. Don't then equate loneliness with a frozen cornfield, a goose separated from the flock, and a teenager waiting at the punchbowl while others dance. Finally, keep any symbolism or figurative language in the background. Ideally, figurative imagery makes literal sense as well; it functions on two levels.

Duplicity

In everyday conversation, duplicity refers to deceit, often because a two-faced person says one thing while meaning another. As a literary technique, duplicity also involves two distinct levels of intention; the image operates on literal and figurative levels simultaneously. Any element of deceit refers to the possibility that certain readers detect only the literal message.

Language offering both literal and symbolic meaning develops the storyline while adding an additional layer of richness. Contrast two familiar examples. *It's raining cats and dogs* functions only on a figurative level. People realize that this represents torrential rain, yet the image doesn't correspond with anything from literal reality. In contrast, *Don't count your chickens before they're hatched* operates both literally and figuratively. Figuratively, this expression means that no one can predict the future. The literal meaning makes equal sense: only certain eggs produce offspring. This adage operates literally, figuratively, or both.

When you blend the hidden level of meaning into the scenes of your fiction, the symbolic significance disappears within the storyline. Readers following only the literal meaning remain absorbed in the fictional world, while others discern less obvious nuances. Whether or not readers identify a hidden layer doesn't matter so long as the fiction makes literal sense. Duplicity protects writers from worrying whether readers will find the figurative references either painfully obvious or incomprehensibly subtle.

The following narrative describes one woman's efforts to cope. How does duplicity enrich this portrayal?

"Mrs. Dunbar" — by Helen Dyer

Sarah Dunbar climbed the stairs to her small room and sank into its only chair. She removed her coat, picked up a brush, and carefully stroked the coat. She held it in front of her. Satisfied that she'd eliminated every speck of the day's accumulation of grime, she arranged the coat on a hanger, buttoned the top button, and then hung it in her closet along with one suit and two dresses. Taking off her dress, she repeated the process. Moving each hanger, she made certain that no garment touched another.

Exhausted, Sarah lay down on the bed. She had cleaned three houses that day and was proud of her reputation as efficient and thorough. She wasn't unhappy, but every evening, after her day's work, when she could relax, she remembered how things used to be.

Sam had been a good husband, devoted to her. He cared about his community and often contributed his services. He showered Sarah with everything a woman could want. Together they had planned the big, beautiful house, and she remembered the day they moved in. He had carried her over the threshold as if she were a bride. The city council honored Sam by naming the street in front of their house Dunbar Avenue. Sam had been proud. Nellie was born there, and nothing had been too much for their little darling. When she was three, their wonderful life changed forever.

One afternoon at the bank, Sam had a heart attack and in what seemed an instant, he was gone. She grieved for her beloved husband, and later she grieved because he was not the man she had thought. Bank examiners discovered thousands of dollars missing. Sam had embezzled for years. The bank took away their beautiful home and everything Sam had lavished on them. They were in disgrace. Sarah and Nellie left the house with their clothes in two suitcases. They had nothing else.

Nellie grew out of her clothes, and Sarah packed them away. Nellie graduated from high school with a full scholarship. She was married now with two precious children. Sarah longed to see them. She seldom did.

Sarah watched her figure and could still use the clothes of that other life. Forty years later, she still wore the same three dresses and one suit. When she cleaned the beautiful homes of other people, she protected her dresses with aprons, and when there was a tear or a worn spot, she painstakingly patched.

That other life was long ago. Sarah turned her face to the wall and weary, fell asleep. Morning came too soon. She eased her aching bones out of bed, splashed cold water on her face, and chose one of her dresses. She buttoned every tiny button, placed her only hat on her head, the feather sticking out the side, and glanced in the mirror. She felt impeccably dressed. Sarah closed the door behind her, walked a few steps and made a right turn on Dunbar Avenue. Shoulders straight and head high, she walked rapidly on.

Nothing here necessarily signals symbolism. "Dunbar Avenue" could exist anywhere, and anyone can preserve clothes as carefully as Sarah. Yet this piece illustrates duplicity. The name of the street represents the power Sarah once possessed and sheds light on her pride. Does the narrative provide unspoken clues about why she doesn't see her grandchildren?

Every image operates both literally and figuratively. How many cleaning women wear suits under their aprons or "painstakingly patch" dresses with "tiny" buttons? Sarah's clothes and choices mirror her self-image. Her wardrobe represents that other life when she had reason to be "impeccably dressed." The imagery supports the plot while suggesting much about the woman who must clean houses yet holds "her shoulders straight and head high." Without attracting attention, the duplicity adds a layer of meaning.

Writers sometimes complain to me that they don't know how to add duplicity to their narrative. I encourage them to slip on the shoes of a poet, because many poets find symbolism in everything from peeling paint to peeling potatoes. When writers see the world this way, metaphors materialize everywhere. Must every metaphor exhibit duplicity? No exceptions allowed? Not necessarily. Some effective metaphors lack a literal component. That cow jumps over the moon only in our imaginations.

Metaphor versus Simile

Georgina's imagination energizes her like a rigorous swim in a cool lake. This simile compares imagination with a satisfying workout. Similes express non-literal comparisons by including the words *like* or *as*: Peg is determined *as* a cheetah. Metaphors omit the language signaling the comparison: When Peg wants something, she's a cheetah. Metaphors attract less attention and often seem more immediate, thus providing greater impact. Contrast these examples:

Simile

They sat by a lake that resembled a piece of royal blue velvet decorated as if someone had flung strands of diamonds across its surface.

Metaphor

They sat by a lake of royal blue velvet, decorated with strands of diamonds flung across its surface.

PAINTING A BACKDROP

When you add figurative language, question whether a metaphor would better suit your purpose. But no matter how forceful and vivid, provide just enough figurative language to invigorate reader imagination. This applies to the details of setting and atmosphere as well.

Checklist: Setting

✓   Do you integrate setting with characterization and action?
✓   Do you include enough detail to let readers picture the scene?
✓   Do you present only details that contribute?
✓   Do you incorporate at least two of the five senses?
✓   Does any figurative language you use enhance without attracting attention?
✓   Should you substitute metaphors for similes?
✓   Does your fiction provide a sense of atmosphere?

STRETCHING EXERCISES

1.   Integrate setting with character.

Write a sketch where the conflict confronting a character stems directly from a particular environment, such as teaching scuba diving at a resort, sharing a small house with eleven siblings, being confined to one's home, or anything you want to explore.

2.   Use setting to convey intense emotion.

Choose a setting that affects plot outcome, such as a a football stadium, a bus station, a mountain village, or other choice.

3.   Revitalize an overworked atmosphere.

Invigorate a familiar scene, such as a moonlit cemetery, dark alley, beach at sunset, or other location. Rely on metaphors instead of similes.

LOOKING BACK, THEN AHEAD

Because Georgina has fed her characters, especially the insatiable Henry, she's seen them handle dirty forks and grimace over hideous place mats. Georgina plans to transfer this knowledge to the actual setting of her fiction. Setting joins characterization, plot, and point of view as fundamental to her novel.

Along with Georgina you've now investigated these basic elements. At this point Georgina feels as if she can almost visualize her fictional world and detect a plot peeping out from that palpable reality. Maybe she can quit filling her wastebasket with piles of crumpled pages. Yet her present version seems, well, vague.

"Cinnamon! Hey. Leave that bottle cap alone and listen to me. I think something's missing." She tips him over and tousles his tummy. "Do you think readers understand why Henry doesn't call Ashley? Are they dozing over Henry's procrastination or Mrs. Petry's badgering? Cinn, I'd trade you a hit of catnip for advice about what to explain and what to cut." Georgina leans into the soft fur. "You're trying to purr out a message? It's all in the details? Lovely. What's the rule about how many details to include?"

CHAPTER 8: Details

Just Enough Reality

What feels coherent from the inside, from the outside often does not make sense. What a hard truth this is! Most writers have broken their hearts against it. (Friedman, 76)

TRYING OUT YOUR READER'S SHOES

"Henry, why do you like curry?" Georgina reaches across a student union table and taps his shoulder.

"Georgina! I'm studying! Want me to flunk out last semester of senior year?"

"Sure Henry, I'm no friend of yours. I enjoy seeing powerless beings hurtle to their doom. Mayhem, failure, torture—they turn me on."

"I believe you," he says, not looking up from the heavy volume on the table. "Midterms are next week, or don't you keep track?"

"I've got enough on my mind with your dad's business, your mom's volunteer work, and my own job without concentrating on ..."

"Concentrating's what I want to do!" Henry grabs his aqua marker and searches for the sentence he was pondering. As he shifts position, the entire pile of textbooks slides to the floor. "Please Georgina, I need to work."

"I know."

Experienced with these interactions, he waits.

"Henry," Georgina whispers.

He rearranges his books, then looks up into her smile. He grins back. "You're my best friend."

"I should hope so." She offers her potato chips. "Just a question or two."

He sets down the marker. "Get it over with."

"Why would anyone care so much about curry?"

"It's sweet and tangy. Like barbecue sauce, but not gloppy. Besides, the question's stupid. Millions of people, probably billions by now, eat curry every day. Did you know they introduced it to mask the taste of rotting ..."

"That's just the sort of information I don't need."

"Too bad. There's nothing on my sociology test about curry, either."

"Okay, you're free to study—if freedom to study means something to you. But we're not done with your food proclivities."

"We are for the moment."

Henry's right to insist on studying. Unless he knows the details, he won't understand enough to ace the test. Georgina's right, too. Without understanding the fine points about Henry, she won't ace her novel.

Credibility

Novels succeed when readers enter a world as vivid as the one beyond the covers of the book. This can't happen unless writers omit the distractions that interfere at the level of the details. Too many writers conquer structural problems with characterization, plot, or point of view and think they're done. Yet irrelevant or inadequate information weakens the strongest characters or plot.

Your fiction making perfect sense to you doesn't guarantee it making sense to others. The autobiographical details that writers often incorporate can confound decisions about clarity and focus. Some pertinent information about background, characters, and scenes never makes it from the writer's memory to the pages of the fiction. Certain memories, once recorded on paper, defy reader expectations about plausibility.

Writers sometimes balk at altering those details. Yet fiction isn't about transcribing reality. Suppose you share the events of your day with a friend. If you either boast how everyone worshipped your presentation or whine that everyone detested it, your friend might chide your exaggeration. But your friend probably won't threaten, "I don't believe you, so I'm leaving." Readers, however, demand credibility. When they don't get it, they bid the fictional world goodbye.

There's a fictitious world of difference between what can happen and what readers believe. Consider a day when everything fails. You wake before five because a wrong number jars you from sleep. You toss around for hours, then drag yourself from bed but fail to start the coffee. You leave late (without coffee) and get stuck behind a truck blocking a van. At last you're moving. Six stoplights separate you from your office. Each turns red at your approach. Oh no, you're almost out of gas. Has the cashier line ever been longer? The meeting starts while you're en route, and, look, someone's taken your parking space. Breathless, you skulk into the last empty seat in the conference room and trip over your open briefcase. Its contents spill everywhere, without your notes for the meeting, however. Those are on your kitchen counter. And this day just started!

Familiarity

Unless your goal is comedy, incorporating all these details sounds farfetched. Instead, make the actual specifics believable. Omit, fabricate, or fictionalize as needed. Details seem more convincing when you integrate the alien with the habitual (Lodge, 137); this bridges the world where your readers live with the one your characters inhabit. This becomes especially important in genres like science fiction.

Perhaps you portray characters that reside on Mars and require protective clothing outside the space structure. Few readers own space suits, so constructing these of *zyscuphon* provides little for the imagination to grasp. Readers relate to everyday acrylic, a material linking familiar and distant planets. Commonality stems from plastic being an ordinary item we can see, touch, hear, and, too often, smell or taste.

Familiarity reinforces the illusion of reality. Yet writers don't always check their details against that, especially when working from memory. How can you know whether you provide common ground and describe neither too much nor little? Relax. Complete detachment is neither possible nor necessary. After all, without ego, few of us would write. Gradually, you'll improve at assessing your words as a reader would. Gradually, you'll sense which details readers seek.

Context

Readers like feeling grounded. Basic facts about character appearance, status, and circumstances prepare readers to experience tension over the conflict. Such information includes anything from the death of the protagonist's father when she was three to realizing that the protagonist's fiancée has hung up and he shrieks at no one.

Providing indispensable details differs from belaboring the obvious. Who cares that Elinor left the house, locked the front door, walked to her car, opened the driver side, slipped into the seat, buckled her seatbelt, inserted the key in the ignition, pressed her foot to the gas, and pulled out without looking behind her? Does anything except the last detail matter? Eliminate whatever readers can infer.

Some writers ask, "How do I get Elinor out of the house?" If an indoor scene precedes the accident, detail can move Elinor outside while developing the storyline: Pondering the best way to tell Pete that their adolescent daughter was pregnant, Elinor backed the new Lincoln right into the little Toyota cruising past. Effective details often accomplish more than one task at a time.

Effective detail also pulls readers deeper into the storyline rather than farther away from it. So unless you address a special-interest group, exclude material distracting to a general audience. For instance, perhaps everyone in the Kapp family worries whether the protagonist will serve or withhold the *toastwiches* that make your mother's brunches famous. But interrupt the accelerating plot to explain *toastwich* preparation, and readers lose interest. Tasty or not, trivialities irrelevant to fundamental characterization or conflict blur the focus. To distinguish the obvious or inconsequential from the essential, cross-examine yourself about which omissions you'd notice as a reader. Then be honest about your observations.

GATHERING DETAILS

Generating many, many more details than you need increases the odds of selecting functional if not memorable ones. Perhaps you've already contemplated the characters, events, locations, and symbols of your fiction. Whether or not you ruminate at sunrise or sunset, while scouring pots or longing to fall asleep, compile a long list. That's what Georgina does.

"So Harriet, this is your favorite restaurant?"

Mrs. Petry's eyebrows shoot up. "I beg your pardon?"

Georgina flushes. "I said, 'Mrs. Petry, this is your favorite restaurant?'"

"Why yes, dear. Has been for years."

"What pleases you about it?"

Mrs. Petry snaps her fingers for the waiter. "Everything. And my plebian son dislikes it all."

"Why do you suppose that is?"

"Henry's a classic case of rebellion. Whatever I want for him, he rejects." As if swatting a fly, Mrs. Petry waves off the waiter refilling her water glass.

"Maybe. Or possibly he's his own person? Just different from how you hoped your offspring would evolve?"

Mrs. Petry clears her throat. "Absurd. Surely you don't claim to know him better than I."

"I couldn't say." Georgina pushes aside a cracker dotted with watercress and cream. "I'd like to."

Exchanges like this help both Georgina—and her potential readers—understand Mrs. Petry. But Georgina's novel won't necessarily mention watercress. Just as with characterization and plot, only the best details get chosen. (By the way, if you never brainstormed characterization or plot, it's not too late.) Say you've developed a long list. Which factors identify the details that enrich the fictional world?

DEVELOPING DETAILS IN CONTEXT

Choose details that advance the storyline. To illustrate, imagine anticipating photos of your favorite relatives on their Jamaican vacation. You don't care about waterfalls surrounded by tropical foliage; *National Geographic* provides better shots. You await Uncle Merle's grin framed by cascading water and lush flora. Uncle Merle has always feared heights. So his position atop a cliff represents a change in character, which captivates you further. But if Uncle Merle grabs the snapshot and starts pontificating on Caribbean geology or history, your interest flags.

To keep Uncle Merle and his accomplishment central, integrate description with scene. This simulates the real world, where people's actions are inseparable from how they dress, respond to mirrors, and react to snow or heat. But in the wrong place, even the right details leave readers distracted or unsure which clues to notice.

Are you thinking that you needn't plant clues? Murder doesn't occur in every piece of fiction, but mystery always must. Every detail should function like a clue informing readers what to heed. Skilled writers want their readers to proceed carefully and thoughtfully, and careful, thoughtful readers assume that each detail signifies a definite purpose. Extraneous details, however captivating, diminish suspense and undermine the intensity of important ones. By implying a non-existent significance, irrelevant details mislead as well as distract.

Consider this scenario.

Ellie's ambivalent about Ted. He's nice enough but boring. In fact he's very nice and quite well off but torturously boring. Still, she agrees to vacation with him in Phoenix. I'll make up my mind once and for all, she reasons. They hike, swim, and golf; they buy each other small gifts. He has exquisite taste. Ellie couldn't be happier— until she suspects he's about to propose. Why else would he order champagne? Maybe I'm not ready to marry anyone, she broods. Maybe my reluctance has nothing to do with him. They lounge on the patio, sipping from the fancy hotel's crystal goblets. The sky is ocean blue, the bougainvillea shocking pink. More than once, Ted slips his hand inside his jacket. Surely not a ring! Ellie refills her goblet and chugs its contents. How can she prevent this? Her eyes drift to a lizard hiding in some nearby rocks.

Right along with Ellie, readers follow the lizard. What if his long slate-gray tail steals the scene? Readers encountering this reptile four or five times expect significance in terms of plot or symbolism. Then how do readers feel after the lizard stretches, catches a few flies, and slithers away? Or what about that bougainvillea? It's not just shocking pink. It's riotous, profuse, drooping with garlands of color. It conjures roseate spoonbills, tropical sunsets, and mauve aurora borealis. Raspberry-colored fountains of blossom cascade...Florid description distracts from the swelling tension. Does anyone still care whether Ted proposes or Ellie flees?

One or two references to the lizard or the bougainvillea represent pleasurable teasing that involves readers in Ellie's decision. Repeated references, however, bestow undue significance. Similarly, details pinpointing the time of day, the hue of the sky, or the condition of the lawn must remain in the background without announcing themselves. Details that seem random confuse readers.

PRODUCING AN EFFECT

In contrast, precise details establish commonality, and vivid examples can help readers visualize an abstraction like fear, ambition, or alienation. In F. Scott Fitzgerald's *The Great Gatsby*, for instance, the recurrent image of the ash heaps represents dishonesty and carelessness. When writers create a pattern through deliberate repetition, this reinforces coherence. When details suggest a figurative or symbolic layer beyond their literal meaning, this conveys theme.

Whether literal, figurative, or both, your details should blend together, suggesting an ensemble—not a mismatched outfit. Picture someone clad in blouse, skirt, jacket, scarf, and shoes each in a different and thus clashing shade of pink. Some people could find this so distracting that they notice nothing else. This applies to the fictional world as well.

If you focus on significant details and harmonious imagery, you can reveal much in few words, as this example demonstrates.

"The Green-Eyed Monster" — by Ruth Calden

He wanted to yell, "Take your hands off my wife." Instead, Kurt tried to appear calm, as though he returned home every day to discover a handsome male friend massaging Sheila. He decided not to give her any grist for a charge of jealousy. At least not in front of Peter. After all, he could confront her later. "One of your tension headaches, Sheila?"

She sat on the piano stool, leaning forward over a Beethoven sonata, her face in her hands as Peter kneaded her back and shoulders. Tendrils of blond hair escaped her ponytail clasp and cascaded down her peasant blouse. Peter's cello and bow lay aslant on his chair beside the grand piano. Above it, the tenuous rays of the setting November sun stained the windows.

Sheila didn't turn at the sound of her husband's voice. She just froze.

Kurt wondered if she felt too embarrassed to reply? Or was it part of her growing remoteness? Remoteness fanned no doubt by those sessions in that encounter group.

Something in Kurt's voice alerted Peter to trouble, and he cut the growing silence. "Hi, Kurt, didn't hear you come in. Yah, Sheila has a terrible headache. Thought I'd try to help."

Kurt's suspicion melted somewhat under Peter's warm greeting. The guy, graduate school casual in tie-dyed shirt and sandals, certainly didn't look guilty. Kurt remembered that Peter and Ramona seemed happily married. Feeling a surge of love for Sheila, Kurt placed his hands on her shoulders, sensing her tenseness under the blouse.

"Sweetie, any better? How was your practice?"

Sheila smiled faintly and rose from the piano stool. Maybe I misjudged Kurt, she thought. "Great until the last half hour, but then this headache hit."

Beaming, Peter nodded in agreement as he placed his cello back in its case. "Yup, I think we're ready to wow them in Berkeley."

"Berkeley? What's going on in Berkeley?" Just when Kurt felt himself under control, the jagged edge of panic shot upward from his stomach.

Peter drew a letter from a folder. "This came today. An invitation for an all-Beethoven festival. Our first performance outside Wisconsin!"

Sheila put her hand to her forehead. She wanted to shout, "Oh Peter. Not now."

Kurt fought a wave of suffocation. He imagined Sheila and Peter, overnight in the same motel. Deep into an affair. "Oh. Sure. Great news, " he mumbled through clenched teeth. "But Peter...don't count on it. Sheila and I will have to talk about it. Together."

A few details about clothing ("peasant blouse" and "tie-dyed shirt") establish the time period, although the situation remains universal. References to the sun and the musical instruments strengthen the scene by locating the characters in physical space. Precise characteristics show appearance ("handsome" and "tendrils of blond hair"). Particulars about the men's behavior contrast them ("beaming" versus "clenched teeth"). Mentioning Sheila's "encounter group" and Kurt's assessment that this increases her "remoteness" reveals much about this marriage. Only Peter expresses his feelings, but subtext adds meaning to the rest of the dialogue. Every detail involves readers in this interaction, creating a portrait resembling not still photograph but film.

INFUSING VITALITY

Contrast that vigorous characterization with something like this:

The young, gray-eyed man was of medium height and build. His clothes were not striking and attracted no attention. One could look at him and remember nothing about him.

One could read this description and remember nothing about it! Vague, static physical description, either of characters or setting, slows pace. Even when deliberately postponing outcome, interrupt the advancing plot only to furnish something colorful or startling. You probably need less description than you think. Many of us write because we love words and images, yet the chance to visualize character and scene is among the pleasures fiction offers. Leave room for reader participation.

"Georgina, I know that you're a control..." Seeing her face, Henry shifts to, "I've got a question for you."

"Okay." She loosens her grip on Cinnamon, who sees a chance to escape further brushing and flees.

"How do you make yourself do something that you think you ought to but find too scary?"

"You're a little inarticulate, Henry. You mean like changing my novel's point of view?"

"Actually, I mean like much more important."

"More important than my novel? Be specific then. Unless you don't care whether I answer."

"Well, hypothetically of course, say people have been friends for years. Then someone says something that changes the *friends forever* part...is it worth the risk? When there's so much at stake? Do you think?"

Georgina offers Cinnamon half a catnip leaf and resumes brushing as he chews. "Henry, you gotta do what you gotta do." She feeds the cat the rest of the leaf. "I'm taking risks to write the novel I want. I might eat a little too much chocolate in the process, but I'll get the job done. Surely you won't miss out on the happiness that can come from risking change?"

No one cares whether Georgina soothes herself with brownies or peanut clusters. Readers resent excessive or irrelevant description. Is Henry referring to Ashley? That kind of detail matters.

Precision

Georgina's still searching for an image that helps readers picture Henry's dilemma. Gail Godwin describes how the right detail transforms lifeless words into a living fictional world.

> What detail is going to tell you more about the character, move the story along; what detail, of itself—if you're working on a big level—can stand for the reason behind that story? There's that nice literary term, "objective correlative." It isn't very descriptive; maybe we need another term. A detail, an object, something that will say, "This is the essence of the story." The famous one that is given in many creative writing classes is from *Madame Bovary*. On the way home from the first big party they went to, a nobleman flings a silk purse down on the road—am I remembering this right?—and Charles finds it and takes it into the carriage with him, and then she holds onto it and studies it and cherishes it and it becomes for her a physical symbol of the life she wants and cannot have. One detail like that—sometimes you can't look for it, it just makes itself known as you work on your story—becomes significant and helps the reader know what the story is, and their angle on it is. (Delbanco in Neubauer, 132-133)

Godwin is right that the search for the quintessential detail often eludes even the most skilled writers. But seeking image instead of explanation increases the odds of discovering that "essence." Choose details consciously. Once you capture that special detail, it can transport your readers.

Note how detail strengthens this passage.

"The Sauna" — by Sarah Brooks

A shift of bodies creates space for yet another figure stumbling into the dimness and grappling along the wall to the back.

How many people can fit in here, Anna wonders. She sinks onto the bench.

An initiate into the ritual of the sauna, she feels unfamiliar with the etiquette of nakedness. The nudity poses no problem in theory. That she perches next to strangers without a shred of clothing between them seems *de rigueur*. Eye contact focuses conversation above the neck, not below, and the cadence of conviviality comforts her. Anna clothes herself in nonchalance and relaxes.

Someone ladles water over the rocks. The hiss sears the outline of her lips and the rim of her nostrils. She changes her position to knees crossed, an arm slung across her chest, and a hand clasped over her mouth and nose, maximizing protection. A nod toward her seatmates mimes interest, as if to say, "Ah yes, I couldn't agree more."

Anna resembles "The Thinker," pondering escape. She searches for relief from this oven. Spying bundles of twigs in a bucket on the floor, she lifts a bunch with leaves and begins flailing herself. But this offers no protection from the heat. The flicking doesn't cool her skin, and instead of a breeze, the prickle of branches tenderizes the flesh and intensifies the burn.

Another scoop of water is poured. The effervescence skitters across the surface of the rocks like a spider. Anna sucks in a breath that could turn her lungs to ash. Wearing only a necklace of beads of sweat, she bolts for the door and the promise of air.

Most of us associate *sauna* with furnaces, discomfort, and perspiration. This description, however, adds interaction with other participants ("eye contact" and "cadence of conviviality"). The details evoke unexpected sensations: "the smell of ash," "the hiss of the water," the shifting of various body parts ("knees crossed," "arm slung across chest"), and "the prickle of branches." But the two figurative phrases make this piece memorable. Anna dons "a garment of nonchalance." However, it doesn't help; the spider still drives her out the door.

ASSESSING THE WHOLE

The impact of your details stems not from their number but their contribution. Choose them to make your fictional world substantial.

Checklist: Detail

✓ Do you include all the details needed to follow the storyline?
✓ Do all your details add?
✓ Do all your details support the main emphasis?
✓ Do all your details intrigue?
✓ Are your details credible?

STRETCHING EXERCISES

1.   Choose details to heighten reader emotion.

     Delete every detail that tells and replace it with one that shows.

2.   Narrow the focus in a descriptive passage.

     Make every word and image support a single impression or concept. For example, in John Steinbeck's *Grapes of Wrath,* a turtle struggling across a highway symbolizes the human attempt to escape poverty and humiliation. Steinbeck describes the animal's desperation without emphasizing the countryside, the highway, or related difficulties.

3.   Maximize nouns and verbs.

     Portray a person, place, object, or emotion using a minimal number of adjectives and adverbs.

LOOKING BACK, THEN AHEAD

"Henry," Georgina murmurs, "describe your mom's dining room. I can't picture it."

He shudders. "Who wants to picture it?"

"Give me a break."

"Georgina, you can offer me lobster and I won't visualize that room." He winces. "Still gives me the creeps."

"That bad, huh? Henry, I know your mom had all kinds of rules for you. Was the living room off limits?"

"Are you kidding? When I was five I cut my hand falling off my bike. I was bleeding some and crying and muddy. And scared. So without thinking I barged in the front door. She's serving someone those little crackers. I think you call them ..."

Georgina passes him a peanut chew. "Who cares what you call them! What happened?"

"I don't remember exactly. Just my wailing and her pursed lips. Later I got lectured on bloodstains and humiliating her in public. That room was like a temple, and I hated it."

"Okay, Henry. Enough about the past. On to the future. What's your favorite thing about Ashley?"

Henry's disinterest in the snack she offers confirms that he's too far off for further questions. Georgina reaches for her laptop.

Back when Georgina wrote only autobiographical fiction, she fantasized about learning to choose the right details, then never considering details again. Now she knows that her first draft probably won't capture Harriet's living room. Nor is Georgina certain what Henry loves most about Ashley or what readers long to know. Selecting details is a process, not a formula applied to every scene or character from then on. Even without a diploma in detail selection, however, experience with writing and rewriting increases proficiency at grading details and determining which pass or fail.

This process equips you to notice whether you left readers wondering when that character left town or how many people can fit around the table in a room described as tiny. You become more comfortable with what readers must know to sustain the fictional world.

The next step is making characters and setting three-dimensional. Fiction moves readers most when it suggests layers of substance. One could call that weighty physicality *texture*. Georgina reviews the objects in Mrs. Petry's living room one last time. She wouldn't mind owning something in rose Italian marble herself. There's nothing like marble in terms of veining, weight, color...can you feel it? What makes that marble solid?

CHAPTER 9: Texture

The Fabric of Reality

A reader who plunges into a canyon right along with a character responds with both head and heart. (Georgina Raymond)

DEFINING TEXTURE

Someone's in the room! Georgina bolts from bed. Reaching into the corner where she stores a baseball bat for just this purpose, she trips on the jeans and sweatshirt she flung on the floor around midnight. Muttering under her breath, she grasps the bat and crouches against her dresser, ready to spring. She hears only feline feet thumping down the stairs. Georgina clutches the bat tighter. Canines evolved to master these moments. Why doesn't she have a dog? Wait. It's…"You jerk!" she shrieks at Henry.

"It's just me."

"Just you. I was scared to death! I hurt my leg and…"

"Haven't I told you over and over to relax?"

"Then I'd never catch up. Oh man, no point trying to sleep now." Yawning, she gropes for her slippers. "I'm going downstairs. I'll feed the cats, write a little before work."

"Georgina, we need to talk. Please? I just realized that Ashley…"

"Sorry, Henry, I want to write, not chat. Get out so I can change, will you?"

"But I need you." Henry nips off the one nail ready for nipping. "Can't I just turn my back? I promise not to look."

"Absolutely not!" She shoos him off. "We'll talk later. Get a grip, Henry. You're so worked up I can practically feel it."

Can you feel it? Georgina's frightened. Henry's impatient. Their agitated feelings play off each other, and their brief interaction includes physical components: clutching, nail biting, and cat sounds on the stairs. Everything from paws thundering, adrenaline surging, or limestone crushing a landscaper's thigh can fortify a fictional world. If readers suffer the solidity of the boulder right along with the protagonist, that fictional world has texture.

We usually associate texture with fabric. Material seems satiny, *knubby*, or rough to the touch. How does the illusion of depth pertain to writing? The issue is sensory impression rather than fabric, details, or circumstances. Fiction of substance shapes a three-dimensional world where readers groan at the alarm's buzz, stroke the protagonist's silk shirt, or grimace over exhaust fumes from the bus. The details that suggest a physical world create texture.

Some differentiate *texture* from *structure*, or the content of prose, which includes its ideas, concepts, and themes. In contrast to structure, texture adds detail that evokes several of the five senses. But texture offers even more. Readers sense texture through the sensations that imagery produces and the patterns that emerge in the fictional world. A world where readers identify and follow patterns seems more tangible. Plot unfolds on a topographical landscape.

THICKENING CHARACTER AND PLOT

After establishing the structure of your fictional world, you can enrich its texture. Replace stick figures with fleshed-out characters and contrived incidents with cause and effect. This suggests more than one dimension. Even after readers leave that world, its memory can linger, can resonate.

Resonance

Literally, resonance describes the physical act of reinforcing or prolonging sound. In fiction what matters is not sound vibration but the way one moment, image, or character reverberates long enough in reader memory to bounce off the similarities and differences of another moment or image. When enough images resound, readers sense a world rich with connections; again, a world suggesting greater order than the actual one. In fiction, order stems partly from unmistakable parallel, pattern, and resonance replacing a hodgepodge of images. Fiction can order the real-life images that assault us without apparent connection or purpose. Correspondence within the fictional world and between that world and the reader's own gives fiction its texture.

Parallels between characters deepen resonance. Readers find this realistic because the similarities and differences between people endlessly surprise us. For example, fiction set at a car dealership can include one character determined to claw her way to the top while her laid-back colleague sneaks upstairs to follow sports on cable TV. Though these characters seem incompatible, perhaps they share an unusual hobby, like bonsai nurturing. Two other characters seem driven to achieve. Yet one values both career and relationships, while the other never lets work interfere with commitment to family. Echoes among characters, subplots, and themes capture the comparisons and contrasts that often remain unnoticed in the real world.

"Mr. Petry, it's so kind of you to join me," Georgina welcomes him.

He tries to smile, yet for the third time in five minutes, glances over his left shoulder.

"What can I get you? I would have brought you someplace nicer, you know."

He looks behind him again. "Georgina, I don't suppose you realize how potentially compromising..."

"Oh for heaven's sakes! No one will see us. Even if they did, we're just having coffee."

"Makes me uncomfortable."

Georgina sighs. "Well, I'm grateful you're helping me out."

He coughs. "It's not for you. For the boy."

"I see. Well, anyway..."

Mr. Petry stirs a fourth teaspoon of saccharine into the thick, bitter coffee. "Here's the thing. Between you and my well-meaning Harriet..." He stares into Georgina's blue eyes. "You wouldn't repeat this, would you?"

"What do you take me for? We all want what's best for Henry."

"Possibly. The net result is someone always telling him what to do."

"I resent that. I adore Henry, and..."

"I know. But somebody's forever at the poor guy. Believe me, I know how that feels."

This interaction emphasizes parallels between various individuals. Georgina resembles her character Harriet. Both Mr. Petry and his son feel constrained. Everyone's glad to lend Henry a hand with his future. No wonder the guy seems paralyzed.

You promote resonance when all your characters address one issue, such as Henry's future, or when they all face one goal, such as selling the most cars. Try to identify a universal component. For example, not everyone hawks autos. Yet numerous readers can empathize with pitting honesty against income or debating how much assertiveness to display. Shared emotions and struggles encourage reader empathy.

Archetype versus Stereotype

Like universal conflicts, archetypes resonate because they remain uniform across cultures. Archetypes conjure our deepest feelings and most significant relationships—the commonality that makes us human. Figures from folklore or mythology, such as the wise grandmother or questing hero, reflect collective dreams, desires, and fears. They carry layers of richness with them, like a river that suspends more and more material as it advances. Adding distinctive, contemporary traits to archetypal figures can suggest great depth.

In contrast, stereotypical figures seem so flat, so familiar that readers often find them comical. The term *stereotype* originated from the mechanical process of reproducing the identical image over and over. Stock characters and predictable situations stimulate little interest because unlike archetypes, stereotypes oversimplify. Replace stale specimens like the uptight banker or the giggling blonde receptionist. Such examples bore certain readers and offend certain groups (bankers, receptionists, golfers—whoever).

In contrast, characters exhibiting texture reveal the issues underlying standard roles like indecisive husband, benevolent stranger, or brutal villain. Many readers turn to fiction for its truths about human nature. To reach this deep level, always know how your characters feel, even if you don't disclose this to readers. Consider not only what drives your characters at any given moment, but also the feelings and moments that led to this point. To illustrate, in *Father Melancholy's Daughter* Gail Godwin portrays Margaret struggling with passion offset by fear of hurt or humiliation. This complex protagonist faces each new situation with all the emotional baggage and learned behaviors of her past. Among this novel's many strengths is how Margaret's romantic attachment never diminishes her worry over her father, his parish, her religion, or her career.

This conflicting array of emotions mirrors reality. When people fall in love or watch others do so, that euphoria joins the rest of life's patterns and problems. Love makes problems easier to take but cannot disguise them for long. Substituting superficial or manipulative emotions for complexity irritates many readers. Even within the limited scope of the short story, writers must convey reality by presenting the background and emotional ambivalence of at least one character.

When you illuminate the factors underlying character behavior, you circumvent simplistic conclusions. Instead of resorting to language such as *he cries like a baby*, reveal why an adult man behaves this way. Description should emerge from deep understanding of motivation rather than overused phraseology. Replace clichés, because triteness at the level of characterization, plot, description, or language can destroy the most original scenario. Rework stale phrases like *good as gold* or *right as rain* along with didactic conclusions such as *crime never pays* or *time heals all wounds*.

Complicate designs that spring effortlessly to mind (*they lived happily ever after*). Add idiosyncratic (though not inconsistent) personalities and inventive (though not incredible) plot twists. To suggest depth and pattern, confront characters with interdependent conflicts. When Dr. Mahler journeys to Africa to track a deadly new virus, readers watch her combat infection and contagion. Compound this with an airline strike and problems with the local government and the doctor's family. The complexity of Dr. Mahler's situation suggests the tangled difficulties that readers often face themselves. Now the doctor's struggle resonates more deeply. The less you rely on the customary and obvious, the more human psychology you can reveal. If you rehash what everyone can predict, you eliminate the reason to explore your fictional world.

But while predictability irritates, anticipation can delight. Perhaps you prefer traveling minus a roadmap, because you dislike knowing what looms in the distance until you arrive there. You believe that uncertainty frees you to discover unexpectedly breathtaking scenery without worrying in advance about obstacles. You're entitled to this choice, of course, just so you don't inflict it on your readers. Fiction derives richness from clarifying the patterns that seem inconspicuous in the real world. Foreshadowing can enhance these.

Foreshadowing

The signposts indicating the territory ahead clarify the connection between character choices and character fate. In the process, those signposts transform flat ground into tangible landscape. Foreshadowing marks the road by identifying causal relationships.

"Okay, Henry. I've had tea with your mom and coffee with your dad. Want to go for a beer?"

"Georgie, I did it!"

"Had a beer? Doesn't sound worth mentioning to me."

"Don't be ridiculous. I'm talking about Ashley!"

"Tell me, tell me." Georgina squeezes Cinnamon until he leaps from her arms. "Hold on, Henry, I want every detail. Meet me at the Den."

Georgina orders the first thing she finds on the menu. "Okay, kiddo, spit it out."

"You've changed your tune. I wanted to talk this morning when you wanted to write."

"That's it, thanks." Georgina manages a thin smile for the waitress. "Henry, don't toy with me."

He surveys the entire room—slowly. "This morning I felt ready to see whether Ashley could like me the way I like—that's what I wanted to ask you. It doesn't matter now. We're going to Blues Festival. It's a whole weekend of..."

"I didn't know you liked the Blues."

"You don't know everything about me, Georgina."

"I guess not. A whole weekend! You'll have a chance to..."

Henry and Ashley will enjoy ample opportunity to get acquainted on a new level while readers enjoy ample opportunity to anticipate their blossoming romance. To weave a layered tapestry rather than a flat cloth, insert clues regarding outcome. Unless these clues attract excessive attention or reveal the ending prematurely, foreshadowing enriches the tapestry.

Discreetly handled, foreshadowing involves readers in plot as well as symbolism. In *To Kill a Mockingbird*, for example, Harper Lee hints that Boo Radley may seem ominous, but people and things often differ from their appearance. Open your eyes and you'll discern the many mockingbirds surrounding you. Other works warn you to look carefully, because danger lurks ahead. Shirley Jackson's famous short story, "The Lottery," prophesies the horrifying ending through repeated references to fate, the color black, and mob behavior. In each instance, foreshadowing enhances texture. Keep your clues subtle, however. Better that readers fail to notice hints than reject overdone and, thus, intrusive ones.

Character Growth

You can foreshadow not only plot outcome but also the character evolution that emerges from decisions and choices. Then readers can follow how characters mature or remain inert. If Ashley bolsters Henry's confidence, will he discover the courage to confront his mother? Character capacity to change infuses fiction with plausibility and depth. But the scope of your fiction—short story versus novel—controls the extent of development.

Perhaps a novel investigates whether Mike's car accident helps a selfish man empathize with his employees, his wife, his neighbors, his relatives, and his kids. But the short story demands restricted focus. Writers need more than a few pages to capture Mike's rebirth convincingly. Instead, now that Mike has glimpsed his own mortality, can he manage tenderness just once?

CLUSTERING IMAGERY

The way Mike reaches out to touch his wife's cheek can convey that emerging tenderness. But what if, time after time, Mike touches her cheek, holds her hand, buys her flowers, calls her from work, praises her cooking, and lets her control the television remote? Conflicting images distract readers, while variations on one add coherence, depth, and power. Virginia Woolf's *To the Lighthouse*, for example, captures the many meanings that the lighthouse represents. These include stability, illumination, love, distance, inspiration, and art. Woolf's challenging novel would be still more challenging if instead of revisiting the lighthouse symbol she introduced separate images for each abstraction. Images skittering everywhere confuse readers. Form a discernible pattern by shaping and organizing.

How does coherence strengthen the following piece?

"Mary's kids" — by Betsy Alberts

Before Sal ever got out of bed, having been licked awake by two very wiggly dogs, she could tell the weather would be a winter treat. The sun peeked in brilliant evidence beneath the bedroom door. "Okay, Luke, okay Hustler guy. I'm hurrying fast as these old bones'll let me. You're just kids. Remember Gramma's got some years on her."

The dogs danced in crazy circles around the room, waiting for the outside door to be opened. They burst into the sunshine, plunging through the new snow. Delighted, she watched them swirl, jump, push their noses down into the snow and throw puffs of white powder over their backs. Their feathery tails in perpetual motion, they playfully fought and chased each other through sparkling drifts.

She poured some orange juice and sat on the couch where she had a good view of the dogs. Mary should be out there now, playing with the huskies that were like her kids.

This house had been Mary's home a mere five months, but it spoke mightily of who and what she had been. Huge rooms, fireplaces, the glass expanse made you feel like you were in the woods, a part of it. Pictures of huskies, books about huskies, and tiny replicas of huskies were interspersed with little cups, candles, vases and dried flowers. Jon had bought this house for his love. She had left her mark to remind him, as if he needed it.

The couch, brand new, had been Mary's pride. Its colorful Indian design fit this woodsy house. The new microwave Sal had bought Mary for her birthday two months ago was on the counter. A pile of condolence cards Jon received after Mary's death lay on top of it, some still unopened.

With a huge sigh, Sal got up and let the dogs in. They raced to their water. With sad, blue-flecked eyes, Luke watched her fill their dishes. No one could tell her this animal didn't miss his mom. Mary had taken Luke everywhere, though little Hustler hardly got to know her.

Hustler finished his food while Luke still thought about his. He hadn't eaten much since Mary left. She'd sat cross-legged on the floor and hand-fed him piece by piece if he didn't seem interested. Smiling, she'd pat his classic head, and he'd look into her face, his adoration obvious. Now he looked into Sal's face, as though wondering why his mom never came back. "He looks like the wolf on my license plate," she thought, cradling his head. "I wish I could will her back to you, and to Jon."

Luke slunk to the patio door and watched the deer approach the feeder. Some more of Mary's kids, enjoying another beautiful North Woods day she could no longer share.

The dogs in this sketch, particularly Luke who misses Mary so, reveal a woman of patient tenderness; she fed her pet from her palm. Following the textured details, readers look across the woodland living room to the deer outside. Readers watch the husky stare listlessly through the glass. The use of brokenhearted dog rather than brokenhearted husband makes this piece. Everyone knows that a husband can miss a beloved spouse, but viewing death through canine eyes brings contour, light, and shadow to this scene.

The imagery revolves around huskies, woods, and wolves, with too many examples to list. Controlled focus inspires resonance, from the sunshine of the first sentence to the conclusion describing the day Mary will never see. Certainly, a writer can delineate every item in a room and still produce a vivid scene. Yet that effect can seem scattered, yanking attention first in one direction, then another. What if this piece sketched clouds, ferns, cookbooks, and copper pots along with sunshine? The blur of images would distract from what matters. Instead, recurrent patterns create Mary's world. In longer pieces, writers can use such patterns to achieve unity.

Motifs

The device called a motif repeats a key phrase or image to achieve an effect. In Ernest Hemingway's *The Old Man and the Sea*, the fisherman frequently mentions the heroic ballplayer Joe DiMaggio. If you're familiar with Josef Conrad's *Heart of Darkness*, you probably recall numerous references to "the horror." Handled purposefully, a recurring image or symbol can sharpen focus and emphasize pattern. A motif, however, differs from using the word *house* three times in four sentences because you couldn't find a synonym. Perhaps that particular house, like Mary's dogs, embodies symbolic as well as literal meaning. If so, revisit that word or image. But don't overdo. When necessary, revise sentences to eliminate repetition, because redundancy differs from allusions that intensify atmosphere, suggest texture, and hint at theme.

CONVEYING THEME THROUGH TEXTURE

A fictional world that seems multi-dimensional most effectively conveys theme or author viewpoint. For example, without saying so, "Mary's Kids" confirms the kind of legacy that certain people leave behind. Though the events in characters' lives provide the best vehicle for illustrating beliefs, some writers still emphasize conclusion or moral. While focus on texture enriches the fictional world, focus on theme accomplishes the opposite.

Say you want to applaud stoicism and perseverance. One route involves analyzing how your grandfather's life confirms the virtue of hard work. Or you could portray a man spending winters cleaning seeds and repairing farm machinery to prepare for summers sweating in the fields. The second approach frees you to follow where your fiction leads, weaving a textured fabric as you do so. Which version would please readers more?

Imagery that functions literally as well as figuratively further enhances texture, because you develop the storyline along with its thematic meaning. Effective symbols can include objects, events, components of the setting, or even the characters themselves. In Nathaniel Hawthorne's *The Scarlet Letter*, for example, the emblem of adultery that Hester wears functions both literally and figuratively. She cannot appear in public without that *A*, which is as visible and tangible as the trees of the forest. Yet the letter also represents Hester's ambivalence about her supposed crime. The embroidery on her breast acknowledges responsibility and community membership. Yet elaborate needlework has transformed a badge of shame into an exquisite ornament. Hester and the image representing her communicate Hawthorne's point about individual versus group morality.

In a contemporary example, the interaction between the characters conveys symbolism and theme in Raymond Carver's "Cathedral." The rendition of the human monument to God that the blind and sighted men draw together represents both literal sketch and symbol of insight that only the sightless man possesses. Readers visualize the interplay between the two characters as well as the design they create. By actively participating, readers realize that the literally blind and sighted characters are symbolically sighted and blind, respectively.

Duplicity

Duplicity suggests more than one dimension. The more readers perceive this in your fiction the better they accept the conclusions you hope they draw. The more universal your symbols seem, the more readers link them with personal experience. Symbolism then seems intrinsic to the fiction and not superimposed. The physicality of your characters and fictional world forms the foundation for symbolism and theme. This is a heavy weight to support, and your characters won't be up to it unless readers find both their personalities and surroundings convincing.

What makes a fictional world substantial as well as credible? Note how detail shapes a textured environment in the following sketch.

"Artwork" — by Jan Schubert

Charles didn't want to be there, but when his mother gave him that look, he resigned himself to another boring evening at the gallery. He hated these fat cat affairs filled with those that talked the right way, dressed the right way, were the right people to be seen with. Nearly every weekend his mother pulled his leash. He was to charm the dog-faced daughters of her friends, young women who talked only about parties, who was seen with so-and-so, and coming out. Charles wondered, "Why do they still mention coming out parties? Nobody should come out anymore unless they're gay."

He was extracting himself from a group of crones when he noticed someone he'd never seen. He watched the woman weave past champagne and hors d'oeuvres, past pale debutantes and rich matrons drenched in glistening designer gowns.

She is gorgeous, he thought. Like a breathing work of art. Dark chestnut hair draped her face. Her loose sweater slipped to the side, showcasing one bare white shoulder. She wore a simple skirt the color of chocolate; it ended above the knee and covered her slim hips like a warm candy coating. Surrounded by an elite crowd and some of the greatest art in history, she paused. In that moment, Charles felt she put the room on notice: being gorgeous, she didn't give a damn about them or their style. She made her own.

As the woman gazed at the Lautrec in the corner, her dark eyes half-lidded, her lips parted in a sensuous pout, Charles was sure she was the answer he needed. He'd been drowning for so long. Finally, someone had thrown him a lifeline. He awaited his moment, then nonchalantly moved to where she stood apart from the crowd. "Quite an entrance," he said to her. "They're still bandaging the wounded."

This scene exhibits all the textural elements mentioned so far. Several levels of resonance operate. References to pets, food, and beauty all recur. Most significantly, the piece implicitly positions the *Lautrec* and the "breathing work of art" against the protagonist's mother, the debutantes, and their mothers. Schubert divides the room between those who copy style and those who make their own. The metaphor "pulled his leash" provides a concrete image for an abstract construct like a controlling mother. Archetypes, too, appear here, from the mother engaged in power struggle with her son to the struggling hero. He faces more than one conflict: with his mother, her friends and their daughters, and his need to change, perhaps assisted by the stranger.

Foreshadowing appears in the very first sentence, when readers suspect that the protagonist will "be there" after all. Even in this short sketch, all these parallels and opposites establish a pattern with no single detail distracting. Individual components intensify the texture, from the simpering gossip of "the right people" with their faces like dogs to the drape of the chocolate skirt over hips drenched with "candy coating." Characterization and imagery construct an encounter so real that readers wait, breathless as Charles, for the stranger's reply.

REVISING FOR TEXTURE

Texture like this develops through scrupulous honesty about when to cut, add or revise. Bonnie Friedman describes the workshop experience when she first realized that texture emerges from a series of conscious, interdependent decisions:

> No longer was your story something bodied forth in a sort of rapture; no longer was it something as natural and mysterious as your own foot. Now it was revealed to be a series of specific choices: why this phrase here, why that explanation there, was this ending "earned" or was it a bit of fancy eloquence glued on, like a false facade on a house? You couldn't answer. The story itself had to provide all its reasons. (Friedman, 50-1)

You can't interrupt to justify a particular detail. Nor should you need to. The more you consciously assess plot, imagery, and symbolism along with characterization, the more readers view your fictional world as having both geography and topography. Attention to choice of details and resonance between them can produce a scene more substantive than the room where your readers read.

Note the texture in the following excerpt.

Excerpt from *A Deadly Shaker Spring*
— by Deborah Woodworth

The matronly middle-aged woman who answered the bell looked her up and down, as if she didn't allow Rose's sort to cross her threshold. The warm spring weather had convinced Rose to leave her distinctive blue wool Dorothy cloak in her retiring room, but she knew she stood out in her long, loose cotton work dress with the white lawn kerchief crisscrossed over her bodice. As always, she wore her woven palm sugar-scoop bonnet over the white cap that covered her hair.

Rose swallowed her self-consciousness and repeated her request. The woman blinked slowly and drew back into the dark entryway. Rose stepped inside. She noticed the smell first, a dankness from years of too much sweat and too little air, overlaid by the sharp odor of ammonia. She followed the woman through a long corridor lit by a dingy chandelier in which only a few bulbs still shone. The peeling wallpaper was a rich burgundy with a raised design that, Rose suddenly realized, represented naked young men and women gamboling through hills and valleys. Rose did not shock easily, but she felt her cheeks grow warm and shifted her eyes to the staircase. Now she remembered. This building had been a bordello until around 1914, when its customers went off to war. The new owners had never bothered to redecorate. (p. 144)

Even without the many pages of material preceding the passage above, readers sense the physicality of this scene. In these paragraphs from a Sister Rose Callahan mystery, readers accompany a young Shaker Eldress seeking information to explain a puzzling series of events. Rose's outfit, from her work dress to her straw bonnet, makes her easy to picture, and readers see Rose the way "the matronly middle-aged woman" would. At the same time, readers view the matron through the filter of Rose's perception.

Rose's perspective continues to control the view through "the dark entryway" to the room "inside." Along with Rose, readers notice not just the intensity of the smell but a complexity rising from perspiration and stuffiness mixed either with urine or efforts to eliminate those other smells. Because Rose's observations and reactions restrict the view, readers experience surprise along with Rose. Whether cavorting youths embarrass readers or not, they still sense that rush of blood to the cheek. They not only feel that they have been in this room. More importantly, they have visited it accompanied by the protagonist.

TESTING THE FABRIC'S THICKNESS

Woodworth precisely controls selection and pacing of details. Few writers fashion texture like this without scrutinizing every image. A stroll in your reader's shoes helps you assess the moments when you offer too much or little. How would you appraise your own pages if you encountered them in a bound book instead of on your computer screen or stacked by your side? Which sections seem sparse or overdone? Is a scenario flat and featureless, or does it exhibit creases and protrusions? Keep weaving until the fabric of your fictional world achieves the desired thickness.

Checklist: Texture

✓   Does your fiction offer vibrant characters, situations, and wording?
✓   Do your images work in unison instead of clashing?
✓   Would foreshadowing enhance your fiction?
✓   Do characters, incidents, and images resonate?
✓   Can readers detect a pattern in your fictional world?
✓   Do concrete examples give abstract ideas a physical presence?
✓   Do you tap into universal images and symbols?

STRETCHING EXERCISES

1.   Sow the seeds of disaster.

     Everyone loves mystery, so this can prove useful even to those not creating *whodunits*. Hint at a small problem that will become a big problem later. Generate tension through foreshadowing.

2.   Develop a single image.

     Confine all the details to one literal or symbolic sensory impression. Choose sunrise, rain, a character's loneliness, or anything you like, but stick to variations on one image.

3.   Repeat a particular word or image for emphasis.

     Present a character, scene, or mood through reverberation and repetition. Use a sound, color, or object to create an effect without irritating.

LOOKING BACK, THEN AHEAD

"Henry, how do you like my new velvet jacket?"

He looks up from absentmindedly shaking a third teaspoon of pepper into his soup. "What?"

"I asked about my jacket."

"Birds of a feather."

"What? My jacket has nothing to do with birds."

"Oh. Your jacket. I was thinking that she said…"

"Well, you're obviously uninterested in me. Ashley called you two 'birds of a feather'?"

"No, I did."

"Yes, I can imagine. Think you have enough pepper in your soup?"

Soon Henry's soup will be thick enough to slice—and to fascinate readers. Texture like that brings a fictional world to life. You can compare texture with the beadwork on Georgina's velvet jacket: an extra something beyond the good fit and solid material of characterization, plot, and setting. Fiction lacking texture seems skimpy and not necessarily worth reader time. When appropriate stitching and innovative design underlie the finished product, readers detect weight and intricacy. If you attend to the essentials of dressmaking or fiction, texture develops from the quality layering underneath.

Yet you don't want readers noticing detail that should serve character and story. Texture must disappear into the whole, or the threads just seem superimposed on top. Georgina finds it easier to suggest depth because of time spent sipping beverages with Ashley, Henry, and his parents. Once Georgina believes that her fiction has substance, she's less likely to pad.

These days she cuts unnecessary words as gleefully as she originally inserted them. After all, she wants to please her readers. Readers respond negatively to writing that's belabored, augmented, aggrandized, slowed down, weighed down, blown up, beefed up, botched up…How did Georgina learn to love cutting her own precious words?

CHAPTER 10: Revision

A Shapelier Reality

Revision is mostly compression—frying the fat out of it. (Peter de Vries in Watt, 26)

REDUCING

"You've put on weight, Georgina," Henry observes, admiring his unbitten fingernails.

"You're the one who eats nonstop." Surveying herself in the bedroom mirror, she muses, "Maybe I could exercise." Georgina checks her silhouette. "Not bad, but..."

"Ashley says Americans view food as symbolic. They..."

"Ashley, Ashley, Ashley. You're no fun, Henry. Are you moving too fast? Why not check things out before you decide what's perfect. Your mom says even as a kid you walked straight ahead, oblivious to tripping, stumbling, getting lost in your thoughts." Georgina eyes the bag of cookies on her dresser. "One day you'll walk right off the end of the pier."

"Think so? Guess keeping a foot on the dock couldn't hurt. I feel so secure with Ashley, though."

Georgina snatches a small cookie and gulps it down. "Everything good takes effort."

"Why, Georgina, I'd no idea you could be sanctimonious."

"Sorry." Seeing his grin, she resumes. "You seem so happy. I just don't want you getting hasty or careless. Another thing, Henry. You've heard that less is more. Want the truth?"

"Any chance of escaping?"

She shakes her head, then stifles a yawn. "Tell me how wonderful Ashley is one more time and I'll—I'll fall asleep."

Repetition and verbosity eventually bore. Condensing demands extra exertion, but that kind of revision distinguishes professional from dilettante. With language or muscle tone, tautness demands regular workouts, paring back, controlling emotional impulses, and monitoring goals.

Self-control must temper the hunger to relate a story or share an insight. Too often, writers rush to convey their cutest, catchiest, *charmingest* clincher or to accumulate a stack of pages. The latter propensity originated in elementary school. Bored with the assignment to compose at least 200 words on summer vacation or another subject someone else chose, we padded, then paused to count. Some students (including some who became writers) marked our rough drafts (18, 56, 108) in between flinging verbiage at that goal of 200.

Some writers counted their way through graduate school. Compose six paragraphs; record the words. Write five more; add...If writers keep interrupting to tally, then including filler words—even paragraphs—becomes habitual. Habits cling even when composing from the heart. Insatiable appetite for diction, image, and symbol spawns obese prose. This appetite consumes everything writers crave, clutch, contemplate, add, multiply—anything except subtract.

Do you believe any of these *false* assumptions?

- Deleting fat and gristle to facilitate reader consumption wastes writer effort.
- Like writers, readers love words and savor triple servings.
- Provide variety. (Why serve only mashed potatoes when you can offer baked, sweet, au gratin, roasted, and scalloped?)
- Ideas and images don't store. Serve them now.

Restrict your prose's diet.

TIGHTENING UP

Verbosity flows more readily than brevity. As writer/philosopher Blaise Pascal confessed centuries ago, "This letter is long because I didn't have time to write a short one." (Camp, 462) Though few people waste as many words as the deliberate wordiness below, the passage demonstrates the resulting tedium, confusion, and agony. Which specific problems contribute?

Wild with unrestrained anger, feeling mad enough to be out of control, so sick with rage that she had everything bottled up inside, and experiencing boundless fury, she pulled her arm past her head, then hit, or, to put it another way, smacked him really, really hard across the mouth, lips, and teeth.

He was standing still because he was still too upset to move or speak, looking blank-eyed into her eyes with a stunned, bewildered way of looking. Why would this woman he'd married, his wife, the one standing here in the kitchen with him get it into that head of hers to hit him just because he had said that it was mostly her fault that he ate out with the guys when she knew perfectly well (because he had been repeatedly telling her over and over, time and time again) that too often she didn't have dinner or even something to heat up when he came in the door to the house where they lived after he had been working all day long?

The reason for this, for her being able to throw off quite a punch for a girl, must be all those hours she spent working out in the gym to get some exercise, build up her muscles, and keep herself in tip-top, perfect, teenager-type shape which prevented her coming home at a reasonable hour so that sometimes she could fix a good meal of more than one course—not just the stuff that someone gets out of the refrigerator, puts in a dish, and then sticks in the microwave to heat before setting it on the table and serving it up.

While he was getting his thoughts together for himself, she just walked out, leaving the kitchen in the front part of the house just off the dining room where they stood in silence and going upstairs to their bedroom on the second floor of their house where they lived.

Superfluous Examples

"Wild with unrestrained anger,"
"feeling mad enough to be out of control,"
"so sick with rage that she had everything bottled up inside,"
"and experiencing boundless fury."

Versus

"Speechless and furious."

Telling What You Show

"He was standing still because he was still too upset to move or speak, looking blank-eyed into her eyes with a stunned, bewildered way of looking."

Versus

"Unable to move, he gazed blankly at her."

Word Choice

"Had been repeatedly telling her over and over, time and time again."

Versus

"Repeating."

Sentence Structure

"Why would this woman he'd married, his wife, the one who was standing here in the kitchen with him get it into that head of hers to hit him just because he had said that it was mostly her fault that he ate out with the guys when she knew perfectly well (because he had repeatedly told her over and over, time and time again) that too often she didn't have dinner or even something to heat up when he came in the door to the house where they lived after he had been working all day long?"

Versus

"Why would his wife hit him for mentioning he ate out with the guys since she didn't often make dinner?"

Redundancy

"Get some exercise, build up her muscles, and keep herself in tip-top, perfect, teenager-type shape."

Versus

"Frequented the gym."

Irrelevant Detail

"So that sometimes she could fix a good meal of more than one course—not just the stuff that someone gets out of the refrigerator, puts in a dish, and then sticks in the microwave to heat before setting it on the table and serving it up."

Versus

"Rarely served a real meal."

Unnecessary Explanation

"Leaving the kitchen in the front part of the house just off the dining room where they stood in silence and going upstairs to their bedroom on the second floor of their house where they lived."

Versus

"Left their kitchen."

One could reduce those 326 words to 84.

> Speechless and furious, she punched him hard across the mouth. Unable to move, he gazed blankly at her. Why would his wife hit him for repeating that he ate out with the guys since she didn't often make dinner? For a girl she threw quite a fist, probably because she frequented the gym instead of coming home after work. While he brooded, this woman who served few real meals, constantly accused him, then socked him for complaining, left their kitchen without apology or explanation.

Tight construction conveys emotion and builds atmosphere. Treat words as if each cost $50.

IMPROVING DICTION IN FICTION

Precision combats redundancy. Say what you mean, and you won't need expressions like *in other words*. Do fine distinctions matter? As Mark Twain put it, "The difference between the *almost*-right word & the *right* word is really a large matter—it's the difference between the *lightning bug* and the *lightning*." (Jacobs and Hjalmarsson, 35)

Connotation versus Denotation

Check a thesaurus and you'll find vastly *different* words listed as synonyms. How about substituting *deviant* for *different* in the preceding sentence? That means something *anomalous*! The nuances, or connotations associated with words, prevent interchanging them, even with similar denotation (or literal meaning). Furthermore, readers enter the fictional world with subjective associations. Diction can bridge the gap between the writer and reader or fictional world with actual one. Novelist and poet James Dickey observes,

> Words are a different sort of medium. They are extremely private...you're forming your own inner vision...If I say tree, and you call an image of a tree to mind, your tree and mine would not be the same... (Bruce Joel Hillman in Strickland, 182)

Choose words to align your "inner vision" with your reader's. Does that "lightning bug" sparkle, shimmer, gleam or not quite any of these? Assess etymology along with essence. Thinking about the roots that give words their meaning helps differentiate between them. Precise wording discourages reliance on modifiers. The most apt adjectives and adverbs distance readers from action and interaction, because modifiers emphasize not the storyline but the words describing it.

Sentence structure

Nouns and verbs propel syntax and fiction forward, while adjectives and adverbs impede the progress of both. Unlike modifiers that attract attention, nouns and verbs shape lean, vigorous prose that shows. Minimize modifier use to create concise, graceful sentences.

You needn't count your modifiers or diagram your sentences. But do experiment with sentence variety, length, and rhythm. Notice word arrangement as well as selection. Sentence tinkering accomplishes more than smoothing wrinkles. Revising clarifies thinking, and clearer thinking promises happier reading. Happier reading also results from relinquishing *outdated* rules that forbid:

- Beginning sentences with conjunctions (such as *and, but, because*).
- Ending sentences with prepositions (such as *of, at, to*).
- Using contractions (even in dialogue).
- Splitting infinitives (Trimble, 85).
- Including occasional sentence fragments.
- Omitting perfect tenses (such as *have been listening*).

Sometimes these rules apply. Your fictional world comes first, however, and it cannot survive exchanges like "No, that is not so! You had been indicating that you would no longer have been working fully to complete it by then!" To paraphrase Winston Churchill, there are exchanges up with which readers will not put.

FOSTERING AN EFFECT

Syntax and diction influence reader reaction to the storyline. When everything works in unison, the impact can be swift and profound—much the way people react when they discover more and more features that attract them to another person.

Georgina returns from the powder room to find Henry and Ashley leaning across the table toward each other. During Georgina's absence the waiter brought the soup, but neither Henry nor Ashley noticed. Georgina greets the couple. Again, though, they don't notice.

"Ashley," Henry murmurs, "I love it that you're a writer."

"I'm glad, because I can't change that for anyone. But why do you like it?"

"Your forehead furrows when you're thinking. You mutter aloud when you reread what you wrote. This dreamy, veiled expression comes over..."

Georgina picks up her spoon. "Soup's getting cold."

Henry lets go of Ashley's hand. "Georgina! I didn't realize you were back."

"Yes. I noticed."

Evidently Henry can only attend to one writer at a time, and Georgina can't compete. Ashley is assured of Henry's attention, but other audiences are more demanding. Effective diction and syntax foster audience involvement, as the following passage illustrates.

Excerpt from "South of Quincey" — by Frank Lusson

Faith Lund saw Ben's jaw muscles tighten, relax, and clench again. They used to talk about the farm after breakfast, but not anymore. Today he just stared through the screen door at the shaggy beef cattle in the feed lot and the stunted yellow corn nearby. Gray fog hung over the field, and black flies had a death grip on the screen. The orange farm cat crouched on the stoop while a fly bedeviled his scabby ears.

"Beef prices are at an all-time low, with many farmers facing bankruptcy," the kitchen radio droned. "Extensive flooding has ruined the crop in western Illinois again this year."

Ben stared at the fog, which was thickening. Faith recalled how he had described their future on this rich farmland. When he convinced her to leave the city, he hadn't counted on five years of flooding. "My God," he muttered, "if you can't raise corn in Illinois, how can you live?"

"In the stock market yesterday," the radio announced, "the Dow was up a hundred points. Bill Gates, head of Microsoft, is now worth ninety billion. His new house will cost fifty million."

Ben winced, shut off the radio, and went down to the basement. Faith noticed that the fog now obscured the feed lot. She could see nothing beyond the cat.

A few minutes later a blast shattered the heavy air. Faith's eyes closed, and she shook her head. She could picture Ben in the recliner, one shoe off and a toe against the shotgun trigger. With eerie calm, she pulled the phone to her and dialed 911. "It's a suicide. The Ben Lund farm, south of Quincey on M by the river. The white buildings. I think he's dead." She hung up. Guilt crept in. She had felt this coming but couldn't seem to stop it.

The basement door opened, and Ben's arm pointed toward her. From his hand dangled a dead rat. "Nailed the bugger. Must have come up from the river and got into the potato bin."

The opening of this short story depicts two characters, captures the history of their relationship, builds tension, and contrasts hardship with excess and determination with resignation. In the very first sentence, the wife's reaction to her husband generates conflict. Rather than attracting attention, the exposition ("they used to talk about the farm after breakfast, but not anymore") develops the storyline and reinforces the somber mood.

Strong verbs propel the action forward: "bedeviled," "winced," "droned," "obscured," "shattered," and "dangled." Few adjectives appear. All are unusual and crucial for creating atmosphere. The corn is "stunted" and the fog "gray." The cat has "scabby" ears and breathes air that is "heavy"—not only with moisture but with the tension in this house and the countryside surrounding it. The phrase "tighten, relax, and clench" describes "Ben's jaw" and echoes the pattern that these lives have followed for some time.

Most of the literal images have symbolic overtones as well: the flies represent decay, the fog obscures the real truth, rats have invaded the farm, and in an adroit stroke, Faith has lost hope. What she and Ben shared has disappeared because "she could see nothing beyond the cat." Hearing a shot, she wants to believe that this represents her way out. Skillful use of language, duplicity, and motif establish resonance, heightening the irony and poignancy.

PAYING ATTENTION TO LANGUAGE

Individual word choices matter. Ernest Hemingway related this anecdote about diction:

> One time my son Patrick brought me a story and asked me to edit it for him. I went over it carefully and changed one word. "But, Papa," he said, "you've only changed one word."
> I said: "If it's the right word, that's a lot." (Winokur, 237)

Good writing stems from insistence on "the right word"; language influences reader involvement with the fictional world. Writers may devote hours to one "right word" after another, but diction must still seem artless. Successful wording remains invisible except under the closest scrutiny. Like the lath beneath the walls, diction that fulfills its role never bulges through the structure. Writers who hope to *sound good* usually end up sounding contrived. Disguise your phrasing and technique as cleverly as your symbolism. Aren't your readers worth it?

STRETCHING EXERCISES

1.   Use figurative language to reveal a character concisely.

Build a character from a figurative image. In this instance, choice of metaphor (non-literal comparison minus the disclaiming *like* or *as*) or simile (non-literal comparison with *like* or *as*) doesn't matter. If you like, start with examples like these:

The blood in her veins flowed stocks and bonds.

Those hands on the plow seemed part of the machinery.

She closed the sewing box slowly, reluctant to leave her finger outside.

2.   Delete ardently.

Try cutting one or two pages of your fiction by at least one third. What have you gained and lost?

3.   Revise with ruthless objectivity.

Question every aspect of your fiction. The sample list below and the checklists within chapters cultivate ruthlessness.

Sample List of Revisions

- Make the title more original.
- Cut the first three paragraphs in order to get right into the story.
- Alter character names to reflect their regional background.
- Reveal character appearance through their comments about each other.
- Collapse the minor characters into one character.
- Omit the conductor's dialect, which reads clumsily.
- Add foreshadowing that hints at the climax.
- Link the major conflict with the subplot.
- Change the point of view from first person to third limited.
- Omit the clashing metaphors.
- Revise sentences for smoothness and variety.
- Introduce a motif about the trees rustling.

LOOKING BACK, THEN AHEAD

"Henry, can I have a word with you?"

"Can it wait, Georgina?"

"You win. Where do you feel like going?"

"I'm not hungry—just busy. Ashley and I tried the new Chinese restaurant. That opened last month? Very snazzy. Pink tablecloths, ivory chopsticks, tanks of three or four kinds of..."

"You're babbling, Henry. If time is money, then words are. Last call. Ice cream at the Black and White Cow, or..."

"I don't like your threatening tone! Forget it."

"Okay. Get hungrier and hungrier. I'll taunt you with the malt that might have been. You're a struggling student, and I've got a charge card. So don't expect the last word."

He won't get it. The nurturing Ashley has bolstered Henry's confidence. Yet Georgina won't let any character, however confident, drift or babble long. She runs a tight ship, because word choice elicits beaming, giggling, or vocal *aha's*! Or word choice elicits dozing, smirking, or whimpering. Whenever language attracts attention, readers notice hearing about instead of experiencing a fictional world.

Neither that world nor the words describing it should attract attention. The exception is metafiction, where fiction introduces the subject of its own limitations and attributes. Georgina's conversations about the nature of fiction illustrate this.

"Muffin," Georgina murmurs, "wouldn't it be great if I could do anything I want?" Ignoring the meaningless question, the cat settles down to sleep. "Hey, you're blocking the keyboard, and I can't type!" She tickles his ears—a little hard. He responds by nipping her hand—a little hard. "I know. Doing anything you want disregards whoever it's done to."

She caresses Muffin's throat. "Say I use details from my life to shape my fiction. Who cares what happened? Only being credible and interesting matter. Right?" Muffin kneads her lap. Georgina stops stroking. He's hurting her legs again. Besides, she's formulating her next question. "Say I use otherworldly details from my imagination to shape my fiction. Who cares what can happen? Only being credible and interesting matter. Right?" She kneads Muffin's temples. The cat purrs. "Okay, sweetie. This won't be easy. I'll need help from you, Cinnamon, and my lucky writing shoes. But when I'm done, they're going to believe and enjoy my combining of fact with fabrication."

How do writers construct a fictional world by interweaving the details they remember with those that their imaginations invent?

CHAPTER 11: Connections

Accessible Reality

Remember back until you see exactly what it was that gave you the emotion. Remember what the noises and smells were and what was said. Then write it down, making it clear so the reader will see it, too, and have the same feeling you had. And watch people, observe and try to put yourself in somebody else's head....As a writer, you should not judge, you should understand. (Hemingway in Strickland, 25)

HELPING READERS PARTICIPATE

"Georgina," Henry suggests, "why not try the tofu scrambler?"

"Are you nuts? I hate tofu!"

"Ashley calls it a perfect food."

Georgina frowns. "Have you any opinions of your own?"

"What, just because I want you to try tofu?"

"You want whatever Ashley does, yet I can't sense any real connection between you. All I hear about is food."

Now Henry frowns. "We talk all the time! Ashley was 16 when her mother died. You know about that, don't you?"

"Well, Henry, yes, obviously I realize that." Georgina bites her lip, turning her attention to Henry instead of the memories his words evoke.

"Right. I knew that." Unwilling to meet her eyes, he rearranges his silverware. "Changed her whole life."

"Believe me, Henry, I know." Georgina folds her napkin into a fan, undoes the folds, then starts over.

His sharp tone interrupts her thoughts. "How could you know how she feels!"

"Because it happened to me first! I think Ashley needs a stiffer upper lip. That's what I've always sought."

"Ashley doesn't have to do everything the way you do. Anyway, she stands up for herself—it's one of the things I love about her. Of course you cope better." Henry grins. "You're significantly older, aren't you?"

Georgina sticks out her tongue. "Not significantly. And when I was Ashley's age..."

"Sorry, Georgina, what happened to you isn't the issue."

When Georgina writes fiction, the issue isn't her feelings but Ashley and reader response to her. Over tea if not tofu scrambler, Georgina has contemplated how this terrible loss affected her character. The more Georgina contemplates Ashley the more Georgina focuses on the events of Ashley's life. All characters—including Georgina's—deserve to experience their own feelings and roles, which needn't entail being a redhead, New Yorker, executive, or feline fancier. Unless Georgina removes herself from her fiction, how can she originate any character except Georgina? She enters the heads of her characters and her audience. When their needs conflict with hers, she grinds her teeth and puts theirs first.

Georgina reaches her audience by finding the universal in the personal—by making what matters to her meaningful to others. She can't accomplish this easily. If only a magic wand could accompany those lucky golden writing slippers! Slippers and wand help her appraise her memories, emotions, and ideas as if someone else originated them. This helps her discover the element or essence of her own experience that she shares in common with everyone else. Now she can write a novel in place of a memoir. Now she can uncover emotions and truths that mean something to those who don't know her.

CONSTRUCTING BRIDGES

As a writer your goal is to connect your mind with your readers' minds. They must find the material stored in your memory or generated by your imagination tangibly real. Readers participate in fiction when character experience resonates with something that readers themselves feel or recall. Good writers construct truth from fact. Good writers help define reality. Identifying the communal in human experience underlies much of the world's great writing. Detachment plays a larger role in this than universal subjects (the death of one's parents) or point of view (the more objective third person). You need some distance to transform your life into fiction. Willingness to "understand" rather than "judge" helps construct believable, intriguing characters.

REWORKING FOR PLAUSIBILITY

Readers expect fiction to resonate with their knowledge of the world, though at a deeper, richer level. Fiction provides that level by seeming realistic, which differs from being realistic. If you're transforming your personal history into narrative, consider what will convince your readers. As a fiction writer, you gain nothing by insisting, "That's what really happened!" Are you certain you know? After all, your version of truth is one of several. Admitting that memory has already modified events frees you to discard or embroider as needed.

Grant yourself permission to reconstruct your memories in order to intensify credibility, significance, or both. Perhaps you attended your first poetry reading in the suburb where you grew up. Would a Greenwich Village coffeehouse make a better backdrop? Say you want to write about your cousin. To shorten a long, confusing cast of characters, eliminate four of her eight brothers and sisters, possibly fusing traits from two different people into a single character. Maybe college graduation day shines as the pinnacle of your life. Your boyfriend proposed right after you learned that your mother, widowed and lonely for decades, planned to remarry. Perhaps all that good fortune converged on one day. Will readers find that convergence credible?

Perhaps the day was less perfect than you remember anyway. Has time erased both the afternoon cloudburst and tears over leaving your friends? Autobiographical reality often involves preconceived notions. Did you discern your roommate's bitterness at your marrying the man she secretly loved? Naturally, you interpret events from your own perspective. Memory can blur the world's multiple shades of gray into the polarized opposites of black or white. Few people or events represent either pole, so your fiction shouldn't oversimplify into coarse versus refined, kind versus cruel, or those others.

Children often oversimplify. Can you still visualize that neighbor glaring at you across a lawn so perfect that it seemed unreal? How his red face with that one sweaty curl plastered to his forehead scared you. Even worse than the ghosts glowing in the dark! Close your eyes, and you still hear your former neighbor shriek: "Quit that blasted racket. Stay away from my yard or you'll be sorry!" You spent years being sorry about who lived next door.

If you can visualize your neighbor shaking his fist, you may have trouble portraying him. Your goal isn't recording memories but engaging reader emotions. Preserving exactly what you remember won't necessarily accomplish that. Perhaps you want to reveal circumstances incomprehensible to a child. Maybe the neighbor's daughters were hyperactive. He hollered because high-pitched cackling and screeching pursued him even in his nightmares. What if your neighbor suffered painful terminal cancer? Possibly no special justification excuses him. Might you change your recollections in order to develop a character that is neither monster nor victim?

REARRANGING FOR EFFECT

Flexibility about changing whatever needs changing transforms your life into a storehouse of material. Your experience becomes accessible to your readers.

> There's no denying that some reflective writers write mostly about themselves, tracking their thoughts, exploring the whimsical workings of their own imaginations: Vladimir Nabokov. Nancy Mairs. Peter Matthieson. Gore Vidal. But notice also how their best work always depends on an absolutely accurate sense of the real world—not in some vague, generic way, but in all its astonishing particulars. (Gerard, 15)

Writing about any subject, including yourself, requires both "absolutely accurate" details and "astonishing particulars." Memory often needs the boost that imagination can give. To illustrate, consider this day in an unpleasant family vacation.

The Event

The Smiths reach the picnic area, and Timmy, starved for lunch, rushes from the car. Not noticing his sister Lynn behind him, he slams the station wagon door on her finger. Lynn howls with pain. Mrs. Smith grabs her daughter's hand and pulls her toward the lake: maybe soaking the injured finger will help. But they can't get near the water. Mother and daughter run for what seems like miles. They finally immerse Lynn's hand and return to the car, where the parents exchange heated remarks about seeing a doctor. Timmy keeps screaming about lunch and refuses to apologize until his father breaks down and slaps him.

Lynn's finger seems okay, so they forego medical assistance. Lynn and Timmy take turns taunting each other until Mr. Smith offers a bargain. If the kids will behave, they can have Long Island Duckling, a family favorite, for dinner. The Smiths play water games all afternoon, although Lynn won't forgive her brother.

En route to the restaurant, she sulks and whines about sitting up front with her father. Mr. Smith anticipates escape from the car until he discovers that the restaurant lot is full. Muttering under his breath, he parks across the highway. Timmy wants that duck. Despite frequent scolding about looking both ways, he dashes into the road. The rest of the family watches, helpless, as he's hit by a car traveling sixty miles per hour. Hurled into the air, Timmy lands on his left leg.

The ambulance attendants arrive and confirm that the leg is broken. Now the Smiths visit the emergency room.

These details merely report reality. In fact this sketch describes an actual day. Life, however, isn't inherently probable, exciting, or meaningful.

More Credible Detail

Fiction relies on what readers trust—not what happened or could. This emphasizes the expectations we share in common. "If you want to be true to life," John Fowles reminds, "start lying about it." (Winokur, 8) To unleash the true power of personal experience, omit, fuse, or fabricate as needed. For example, some readers might dislike the humdrum name *Smith*. Would *Petry* work better? Certain details from the above incident might block reader entry to the fictional world. Are two accidents on the same day one accident too many? Which alterations might make this chain of events more believable?

"They can't get near the water" ...*to*... lake access.

"Refuses to apologize" ... *to*... some remorse.

"Slaps him" ... *to*... reasons with his son.

"Exchange heated remarks about seeing a doctor" ... *to*... X-rays.

"Mr. Smith offers a bargain" ... *to*... Mr. Petry punishes them.

"Long Island Duckling" ... *to*... pizza.

"Parks across the highway" ... *to*... parks in an adjacent lot.

"Sixty miles per hour" ... *to*... forty miles per hour in a zoned area.

"The leg is broken" ... *to*... extensive injuries.

"The Smiths visit the emergency room" ... *to*... one accident a day.

More Intriguing Detail

Evaluating what to change begins the transformation that connects one person's world with another's. Fiction readers want to be captivated as well as convinced, and unedited accounts often resemble journal entries. Unless the journal belongs to a famous person, it may relax readers straight into sleep. An ordinary picnic area can seem dull; the Caribbean might heat things up. What could make the incident more surprising or significant? Would fusing material from separate events help? The following versions represent two among numerous possibilities.

> "The Smiths reach the picnic area" ... *to...* The Petrys, who are recovering alcoholics, arrive.
>
> "Finger seems all right" ... *to...* finger is broken.
>
> "Exchange heated remarks" ... *to...* weigh divorce.
>
> "Ambulance attendants arrive" ... *to...* ambulance attendants reject them for lacking insurance verification.
>
> *or*
>
> "Starved for lunch ... *to...* starved for attention.
>
> "Exchange heated remarks" ... *to...* re-evaluate their marriage.
>
> "Watches, helpless" ... *to...* realizes what her brother means to her.
>
> "Visit the emergency room" ... *to...* an obviously unsanitary hospital.

Can you change too much? Yes. Transforming every detail can prove as ineffectual as changing none. If you feel uncertain whether you appease your memories or your audience, ask a reader. If you don't have a live one, imagine where the connections between a writer and a reader might break down. What seems unbelievable or boring? This helps identify which facts to preserve and which to remodel or invent.

MERGING FACT AND FICTION

Protect the storyline—not the supposed facts. Ideally, even readers familiar with a writer's biography can't differentiate authentic details from those resembling them. In fiction, so long as readers detect verisimilitude, guarding the actual truth needn't matter. For example, Ernest Hemingway sets his short story "Big Two-Hearted River" near the Michigan town of Seney. Does it matter whether this place exists? Readers don't necessarily care whether Hemingway camped there, used the actual name, or invented one. (Rumor hints that Hemingway fished the Little Two-Hearted River and refused to disclose the best fishing hole.) Perhaps the protagonist represents the author or another real person who preferred canned apricots to pears—but perhaps not.

Readers care only that the main character copes with shell shock by maintaining meticulous routine when preparing coffee or making dinner. Nick uses meaningless ritual to curb turbulent emotions. The story's details about the can opener and the campfire convey perceptions more significant than bona fide facts. Accuracy sometimes interferes with revealing the deepest truths and connections.

The following portrait derives power less from adding or changing than winnowing and accentuating.

"Meta White" — by Judith Gaskell

Every summer, like a huge mother eagle, my grandmother descended into my young life to carry me off to her cottage on Loon Lake. That cottage was musty, dusty, and just plain old. It had neither water, electricity, nor much else to recommend it. Except grandma. She was the cabin, and I was there to learn everything she knew.

At the cabin I had to use the privy. Nights even the trees looked mean, and great black bears came to mind. But when I asked for company, she'd answer, "Piffle. Nothing out there isn't more afraid of you than you of it." Then she'd add, "There's always the bucket by the back door." Yuck! She knew I'd never use that.

Grand things at night made up for the privy. I felt delicious when she called out, "Get your swimsuit, Sis. Moon's bright." We'd walk that old lane to the lake. Grandmother pushed away from the tumbledown dock and began rowing, the curve of muscle in her arms playing against the rusty red boat. At the right place she'd stop, and I'd slip into the silent water and quietly stroke around the boat, losing myself in the moonlight. When I was ready for the world, I'd pull myself in, shiver a few shivers, and let Grandma wrap me in a big red towel. Then she'd whisper, "Let's sing a row row. See what we can wake."

In repeat rounds, we bellowed to the moon, giggling, until exhaustion set in. One of those moonlight times I first prayed she'd never die. My plan was to become a nurse so I could make her better no matter how sick she got. Even then I knew I couldn't grow up without her. After my prayers, I'd roll over for sleep, looking forward to morning.

Sometimes that brought the deadly words *blueberry picking today*. Blueberry picking! The leg-numbing crouches over eternal fields of blueberries, the relentless sun and runaway sweat sliding into every crevice of your body, the kamikaze mosquitoes removing your life blood. I'd fake deafness even as I heard the clang of metal buckets being plunked on the oilcloth-covered table. "They're picking behind Old Man Abel's. Let's get going, girl."

Since we were isolated, I never figured out how she got these news flashes. "Have to be early, like the Lord would want." The Lord propped up Grandma's plans whenever she sensed audience reluctance. It always worked.

One blueberry-picking day, her flapping coveralls swishing bugs and itchy things into my face, her farmer boots breaking a path for me, she turned. Squatting in front of me, hands on my shoulders, she whispered, "I will never leave you." Then she folded me into herself. Even then, I knew that was all I ever needed.

When writers identify the universal in the personal, they let readers participate in a memory. Focus lets the writer identify the link between one person's experience of love and another's. What if this sketch began by mentioning that Grandma visited with the rest of the family first? That detail would detract from flight to a place with only Grandma "to recommend it."

The world of the cabin breathes for readers because of "the tumbledown dock," "the oilcloth-covered table," and "the clang of the metal buckets." Readers visualize Grandma with "her farmer boots" and "flapping coveralls" and hear her through language like "piffle," "Sis," and "see what we can wake." Description of the privy path or the lake must not overpower the image of Grandma's "curve of muscle." Readers must remember not the experience of "leg-numbing crouches" but the sentence "I will never leave you." Sometimes writers sense which material to emphasize—but not always. The trick is fashioning a fictional world that stirs readers as deeply as their own memories.

Strange Landscapes

Using details from memory and imagination, fiction writers connect readers with worlds they can see, accept, and somehow find familiar. "I suppose I am a born novelist," wrote Ellen Glasgow, "for the things I imagine are more vital and vivid to me than the things I remember." (Winokur, 194) Many fiction writers work primarily from imagination. How do they get readers to swallow their inventions?

Some of the early novelists linked remote fictional landscapes with the familiarity of home. Authors like Mary Shelley and Emily Brönte constructed their novels to make otherworldly characters and situations seem plausible. *Frankenstein* (1818) traces the fate of a scientist who creates a living being from parts of corpses raided from graveyards. Yet Shelley opens not with fantasies about harnessing electricity or originating a new race but with a ship captain's letters to his refined sister. Readers can relate to letters and emotions that resonate with the ordinary world. Shared references help readers accept a November night when two years of research conceived a gigantic being with black lips and yellow skin.

Wuthering Heights (1847) also asks readers to suspend disbelief. Like Shelley, Brönte positions paranormal events in the most credible context possible. Here love lasts beyond death, continuing to smolder while haunting the living. The novel opens from the first-person perspective of the nondescript Mr. Lockwood. The questions that this newcomer poses establish a conventional world. In response to Lockwood's curiosity about his neighbors, matronly household servant Nelly Dean fetches her sewing and narrates her version of the impassioned romance and its consequences. The wild, unlikely ghost tale seems more convincing because it comes from the mouth of the down-to-earth Nelly.

A century and a half later, Chang-Rae Lee combines the mundane with the mysterious in *Native Speaker* (1995). His novel transports readers to the world of secret investigators who reshape the international power structure by revealing and concealing information. This occupation, which pays handsomely, seems distant from most readers' lives. To open with a spy's machinations would thrust readers into an alien underworld. This would also narrow the focus of Lee's book, which examines power in the neighborhood and home as well as the political arena. So Lee begins not with the protagonist's career but with his wife's complaints about their marriage. Her parting note to her husband generates drama, though less drama than plunging into collusion and conspiracy. The empathy that readers experience more than compensates. Again, the key is balancing credibility with intrigue.

Humor makes magic credible in T. H. White's *The Once and Future King* (1939). The wizard is teaching young Arthur, Camelot's future ruler, penmanship. Merlyn orders writing materials from the spirit kingdom. His request is vague, and a newspaper and an unsharpened pencil arrive. Merlyn rebukes the spirits, who then deliver a fountain pen minus ink. The magic of this kingdom functions haphazardly. For all Merlyn's powers, he controls his world no better than White's readers control their own. Merlyn's frustration and the familiar items he mistakenly receives bring a remote realm closer to our own backyards. Details that seem immediate as a daily newspaper matter more than their source in memory or imagination. Linking the familiar with the far away brings the worlds of fantasy and science fiction down to present-day earth.

EXPLOITING UNDERSTATEMENT

The reality your fiction suggests, whether based on fantasy, autobiography, or some combination, must resonate with readers' own. Narrative—not summary—must capture that resonance. The more you call attention to raging emotions the less your readers feel. Do you find the issues in your fiction absolute, devastating, or humorless? That's when you need to show.

Lying on that lilac bedspread, Georgina thinks not about her headache but about her character's frustration.

In her white velvet recliner Mrs. Petry tries to relax with the new *Architectural Digest*. Her son, however, has never been so, so— determined. Imagine Henry refusing to introduce this chit of a girl to his mother. The girl obviously isn't good enough. Mrs. Petry dials her son's apartment. "Henry."

"Yes, mother." He doesn't close his sociology text, though he does lower the stereo volume. "How nice of you to call. I point out, though, that this is the fourth time in four days."

"Well, I'm worried about you and that...about you."

"So you've said," he mumbles, underlining a key definition.

"Can you can come home this weekend?"

"Nope. Too many tests." He straightens the pile of books on his desk.

Noting the pile of unanswered correspondence on the rosewood table, Mrs. Petry answers, "Too many dates is more likely." She admires how the diamond chips in her new ring catch the light. "I don't want to tell you what to do..."

"Then don't. I promise not to force you."

"Don't ever speak to me that way!"

"Sorry." He underlines another sentence, keeping the text away from the phone so she can't hear the marker squeak.

"Henry, I'm worried about you."

"Look mother, that's where we started. And that's what you proclaimed yesterday and the day before. I appreciate your concern. You won't win this one."

The little chips on her ring flash bravely under the lamplight. "I'll talk to you tomorrow."

"Yes, I know. Bye." He doesn't even complete another paragraph before Georgina's entrance.

"You hungry?" she wants to know.

"Not really. My mom called again, and I have to finish this chapter so that…"

"You want to study and sleep. I should leave you alone, because you'd like a good night's rest." Georgina peers at his eyes. "You look tired. Not your usual smashing self."

"Georgina, you have more control over how I look than you realize."

She smiles smugly. "I know."

"Then why do you keep showing up?"

"I miss you." She tries not to whine, yet they both hear it.

"Maybe. But we both recognize your real motive."

"You promised to keep one foot on the pier," she reminds.

"Who says I haven't?"

"Henry, how often do the two of you…" She flushes. "I mean, er…are you studying enough?"

He doesn't respond.

"I'll keep my foot in my mouth," Georgina offers, "if you keep yours on the pier."

"That's already the case." He leans toward her. "Haven't you ever been in love?"

"Of course! I…"

"Then what do you think you're doing?"

Henry will follow his heart. Still, he's likelier to heed Georgina than Mrs. Petry, because Georgina at least feigns playfulness. No matter how luxuriant or powerful the language, telling rarely elicits the desired response from any audience. Georgina might get Henry's attention by describing her own experience. Trying to control him, she'd lose it.

KEEPING YOUR DISTANCE

Perhaps Henry worries Georgina because the ending of her first relationship devastated her. The more passionately a writer feels an emotion or problem, the more vigilant that writer must remain. Most audiences dislike overstatement, clichés, and disproportionate response. What if Georgina's first version of Ashley being jilted came out like this?

> Oceans of unrestrainedly bitter lamentation swelled like a turgid river, then streamed relentless as a tidal wave down Ashley's already tear-ravaged face. Her eyes stung and her throat ached from the hours of crying. But she made no effort to stop weeping or wipe the tears soaking her collar. Ashley never knew she could experience such stabbing pain. "Mike, Mike," she gasped out in tortured bursts of emotion. "If you don't stay with me, I don't know how I'll make it through the rest of my life." The sobs and wails continued. Trembling, the pitifully anguished teenager hungrily clasped her boyfriend's muscular arm, pressing it against her own pathetically wet cheek. "Please don't leave me," she moaned. She'd already lost her mother. Now she would lose Mike! Life wasn't fair! She felt the world ending! How could she live without him? Who'd want to?

In this passage telling, manipulation, and overt sentimentality diminish compassion for a teenager who has lost her mother. In this early draft, analysis, overstatement, and judgments separate readers from Ashley's experience. Even the many people familiar with unrequited love experience little empathy, because overblown, abstract language blocks participation. Readers ordered to feel heartsick or outraged only feel irritated. As popular novelist E.L. Doctorow reminds, "Good writing is supposed to evoke sensation in the reader—not the fact that it's raining, but the feeling of being rained upon." (Winokur, 132)

To convey that, Georgina could let events speak for themselves:

> Ashley couldn't stop crying. "Mike, I don't know how I'll make it without you." She pressed his hand against her cheek. "Please don't leave me." She felt her world ending. She'd already lost her mother. Life wasn't fair.

Let the power of the situation speak for itself. Particularly when dealing with events related to your own life, don't explain, oversimplify, or shout. Whispering reaches a larger audience and leaves a more lasting impression.

In James Joyce's "The Dead," characters rather than author address the sorrow and despair associated with death. Instead of commenting, Joyce describes the snow covering the tombstones in the churchyard, the cabs in the streets, and the people returning from a party. He suggests that beneath the snow blanketing everything, everyone shares secret pain they feel unwilling to expose. Joyce not only *shows* these feelings but taps into universal responses. Hint at deep emotion rather than drowning readers in pathos. Understatement achieves more.

OPENING DOORS FOR YOUR READERS

At its best, fiction lets readers experience what they've never felt and identify the unexpected connections between themselves and others. This happens when the writer focuses not on the raw material of emotion, memory, or personal history but on the narrative. The goal of writing is "not a turning loose of emotion, but an escape from emotion; it is not the expression of personality, but an escape from personality." (Eliot, 58) Turning your emotions and individuality over to your characters involves risk, of course. You never know when your characters will take over.

Georgina finds Henry and Ashley on the couch. "C'mon you two. Let me buy you a fancy dessert."

Henry's eyes never leave Ashley's face. "Not right now, Georgina."

Georgina stretches her legs. The sight of her lucky gold writing shoes perks her up. "Please Henry, just a quick one."

Ashley uncurls her fingers from Henry's shirt collar. "Ummm, a little later, Georgina." Ashley's fingers return to his collar.

"Henry, there's this new place I went with your mom and dad. He said..."

"Georgina, when I say not now, I'M NOT KIDDING, OKAY?"

Poor Georgina. All those pains to become intimate with her characters and now they manufacture their own intimacy. Georgina is a sufficiently committed writer that this pleases her. Besides, she's still got two cats.

Checklist: Fact versus Fiction

✓ Do you value your fictional world more than your memories?
✓ When appropriate, do you modify autobiographical detail for greater impact?
✓ When necessary, do you change details to insure credibility?
✓ Do you avoid oversimplifying characters into *bad guys* or *good?*
✓ Do you understate emotions and themes?

STRETCHING EXERCISES

1. Fuse essential details from two separate experiences.

    Choose two unrelated events and combine material from each to create one credible, intriguing fictional incident.

2. Use familiar details to bring an otherworldly scenario down to earth.

    Which image or collection of images makes a wizard seem like a neighbor or a spaceship like the back porch? If you never write science fiction or fantasy, why not try?

3. Understate.

    Select a tragic experience. Let its power speak for itself.

LOOKING BACK, THEN AHEAD

"Georgina, excuse me a moment, please." Harriet Petry turns to the waitress. "I specifically asked for cream. Kindly take this back." Frowning, Harriet turns her attention back to Georgina. "I presume that you've instructed Henry about moving too fast with this person."

"Her name, as you know, is Ashley. And, yes, Henry and I have discussed his slowing down a little, taking his time. I hope I haven't done anything like instructing him, though he might disagree."

"When I was a girl, people didn't..."

"Excuse me, Mrs. Petry, this isn't about you. It's about Ashley and Henry."

"Excuse me, Georgina. I believe that I was in the middle of a sentence."

No matter who gets the last word, your fiction isn't about you the writer but about linking the world you fashion with the one where your readers reside. Let your characters accomplish this. Characterization remains paramount even with the new popularity of hybrid forms like nonfiction novels. The distinction between fiction and autobiographical nonfiction blurs. Yet one disparity remains. Nonfiction reproduces or explains reality. Fiction, however, needs to suggest reality, often in order to help readers visualize some theme or realization. Such realizations can involve anything from the possibility of love at first sight to the necessity of honoring the environment.

Fiction writers simulate reality while directing events toward a particular outcome. This sometimes involves altering the supposed facts. Without this transformation, readers experience a reminiscence rather than a fictional world. The worlds of fiction spring neither from preserving nor discarding facts. Instead, writers arrange, delete, or fabricate details to help readers suspend disbelief. Artful blending of what could or did happen originates stories more believable and bewitching than mere fact. Ironically, getting beyond those supposed facts helps you to be yourself. You become not just a person with many experiences but a person capable of writing about them. That's a prelude to presenting your dreams, beliefs, and fantasies in the voice that's yours alone.

Turning pages with one hand and petting cats with the other, Georgina rereads chapter eight. Cinnamon rumbles a low-pitched purr, while Muffin squeaks. Georgina isn't paying attention to her cats, yet she can distinguish their individual voices. Looking up from her manuscript, she flashes a Mona Lisa smile over how Cinnamon's voice differs from Muffin's. "Folks who think all cats sound alike are silly, aren't they, baby?" Georgina reflects that her mom, who lives far away and visits rarely, can't differentiate one cat voice from the other. "Unless you live with these guys, you don't know who's meowing."

Voice involves both being yourself and knowing your characters well enough to let them be themselves. If you're missing your voice, can you find it?

CHAPTER 12: Voice

Writer versus Character Reality

You can learn better how to listen to this voice inside yourself. You can learn better not to dismiss it, you can learn not to be frightened of it. You can learn to stay loose enough to let it keep talking and yet attentive enough to remember and record it. When the voice is silent one can only wait. One can only try to keep the channels open, to stay ready for the voice that will come when it chooses to come. (Donald Hall, in Wasson, 349)

DEFINING VOICE

"Should you slow down? Postpone living together?" Georgina pushes little dishes of yogurt and lime pickle toward Henry.

"It's not like this advice is new. I hear you already."

"You're not listening. I bring you to this lovely Indian restaurant, and you're off with—with her!"

"Really, Georgina, you don't sound like yourself."

She glares at him. "I only want what's best for you."

Henry polishes off the last piece of warm, spicy bread, but he's elsewhere. "Ashley always finds the best in people. She has this energy…almost like she leaves a glow."

"Henry, the only glow is in your eyes."

"You don't know her. She's so comforting."

Georgina raises one eyebrow.

"Quit that, it's judgmental. Ashley says negativity gets her down, so I'm trying to be more tolerant."

"I hadn't noticed."

"You're so unfair."

"I'm not." Georgina leans across the table to him. "You're so young and inexperienced. You thought about her a long, long while. But you've only been…"

"I can't help how I feel."

"Can't you hear how childish that sounds? I want to help, Henry. Don't try to resist me."

"Georgina!"

"I didn't mean it like that." She gulps her wine. "You sound like a little boy, and someone's got to watch out for you."

"You're wrong there. I sound like someone madly in love. Georgina, I've never been more myself, and I won't give it up for anything." He reaches his hand across the table to her. "Or anyone."

Between Ashley and Georgina, and despite Harriet Petry, one could say that Henry's found his voice. What is that elusive thing called *voice*? Writers able to sound like themselves have found their voices, because voice involves the singular characteristics that distinguish one writer from everyone else. Your writing voice should echo the timbre of you speaking, thinking, or imagining. Fiction's power comes from the writer's unique sound.

When you focus on the impression your writing makes, your voice disappears inside the attempt to seem worldly, thoughtful, intriguing, or whatever you intended. As Nathaniel Hawthorne put it, "The greatest possible mint of style is to make the words absolutely disappear into the thought." (Winokur, 290) Voice makes Hawthorne sound like Nathaniel Hawthorne—not Jane Austen or Virginia Woolf. An unmistakable voice makes us feel that a writer engages us in private conversation. Unimpeded communication has much allure. Consider all those encounter groups and psychiatric services designed to let people say what they feel and hear what's been said. We want to get in touch with genuine voice.

True versus Counterfeit

Unobstructed sound has no rival. People invest in expensive audio systems to enjoy tone unhampered by fuzziness or distraction. When pure sound comes through, the audience doesn't notice the delivery system. Yet that audience detects inadequate or contrived overtones. You can rework your plot, dig deeper into your characters, and smooth your sentences. But you can't form your voice. You must let it find you, because evidence of struggle sounds contrived. Writing and reading—not struggling—lead the writer toward voice.

Character versus Author Voices

Character voices, of course, require attention.

"Artichokes? On a pizza?" Henry eyes Georgina with horror. "That is not something I would ever eat."

"Henry, you sound exactly like your mother."

"Do not. I was simply attempting to convey…"

"No, you sometimes speak just like her, which isn't a good thing. Gigantic restaurant bills, and I'm still uncertain of your voices."

Henry plunks an artichoke onto Georgina's plate. "I have bad news for you."

"What, Henry, what? I'm already having an awful day."

"Truthfully, Georgina, you sound a bit like my mother yourself."

Georgina grinds her teeth, although her dentist has warned against this. She knows that when the feelings and experiences of writer and character overlap, writers sometimes slip from fictional world into memoir. Every character sounds like the author. Fortunately, familiarity with the inhabitants of a fictional world helps writers preserve authorial voice while developing idiosyncratic ones for individual characters. For example, Georgina's an educated professional who says *between you and I* only when she's had too much wine or too little sleep. Her characters, however, can lack fundamental language skills, because their voices must seem distinct from her and from each other.

ANALYZING VOICE

Where and how do you find your voice? Imitating Charles Dickens, Edith Wharton, or Barbara Kingsolver offers only a starting point, at best. Centuries ago, François-René de Chauteaubriand remarked that "An original writer is not one who imitates nobody, but one whom nobody can imitate." (Winokur, 197) You won't discover your inimitable features in anyone else's mirror. Yet you learn to recognize the features that distinguish you by exploring some of the characteristics other writers exhibit. These features might include

Content: Character development, exposition, dialogue, setting, plot structure, theme.

Style: Syntax, diction, figurative language, tone, repetition, compression.

For example, readers familiar with Hemingway anticipate objective tone, run-on sentences, rhythmic repetition of phrases, and imagery that often functions both literally and symbolically. This style succeeds because once Hemingway matured, he never tampered with his writing voice. William Faulkner's voice is equally striking. His lengthy, complex sentences and esoteric word choices, however, sound nothing like Hemingway. The absence of either voice would leave a huge vacancy in the American literary chorus, which doesn't mean that contemporary writers can resurrect voices from the past to help shape their own. Writers who impersonate other writers sometimes sound ingenuous or satirical.

The characteristics of another writer's voice won't help you. Yet you can benefit from understanding the particulars that compose voice. How would three different writers, each with a singular voice, portray a similar scene?

Excerpt from *Spirit Lake* — by Christine DeSmet

Stumbling on the cinders, Cole quickly scrambled up, shoving the backpack in place. The mementos inside included the papers and a map Mike had left him in the bank. Cole was loath to return to Dresden, a patch of north woods filled with bears...and <u>her</u>.

She'd be a woman now, past innocence. Probably married to the richest man in town, with the big house and kids, volunteering in the church and school. Not involved with trouble anymore.

A muffled click echoed through the fog. A gun being cocked? Or was it only tons of metal adjusting its own weight on the tracks?

If the hitmen didn't splice him, the trains might.

Perspiration trickled down the back of his neck.

Footsteps crunched nearby, planted step by step in the cinders. (p. 2)

How would you characterize the tone here?

This opening scene begins with action ("stumbling," "scrambled," "shoving"), then provides some background material ("loath to return to Dresden...and <u>her</u>") before resuming action and building suspense ("echoed through the fog"). Speaking through the character's thoughts, the author provides some conclusions for the reader ("a woman now, past innocence") while leaving the serious threats unresolved. Does the "muffled click" come from the rail yard or the gun? Can Cole escape both the trains and the hitmen?

The flat tone, straightforward sentences, and short paragraphs build additional suspense. The writer escalates tension with images that evoke several different senses: "cinders," "perspiration trickled," and "footsteps crunched." This scene occurs early in the novel, but DeSmet has already established a foreboding atmosphere. The details of the setting are real and immediate, creating an effect that resembles a film.

This next scene treats similar subject matter from a closer vantage point.

Excerpt from *The Year of the Buffalo* — by Marshall J. Cook

The squealing of tires drew him out of his reverie. He turned in time to see a car barely negotiate the bridge he had just crossed and shoot down Main, straight toward him, going at least 50 miles an hour faster than the narrow street warranted. Bruce stepped closer to the building.

The car, a battered, rust-gutted Dodge two door with at least six large male bodies rammed into it, wobbled with speed as it shot down Main.

"Hey, up yours, old man!" one of the teenagers shouted, leaning out the window of the front seat, passenger side, and giving Bruce the finger.

Must be from Darlington, Bruce decided, having failed to recognize any of Beymer's Hope for the Future among the worthies in the car. Small town Saturday night, still going strong at Sunday sunup. That hadn't changed either. Small towns and testosterone didn't mix well.

Maybe he'd write an editorial on underage drinking. But what remained to be said on the subject? (pp. 13 - 14)

Another isolated individual faces possible danger ("wobbled with speed" and "giving Bruce the finger"). The tone, however, differs significantly, even though both Cole and Bruce speculate on what someone else is thinking or doing. Cole seems restrained, almost neutral ("probably married to the richest man in town"), whereas readers receive Bruce's wry conclusions without censorship ("failed to recognize any of Beymer's Hope for the Future" or "small towns and testosterone didn't mix well").

The character's irony extends not just to the scene viewed from his perspective but to his self-perception ("what remained to be said on the subject"). Readers enter the character's consciousness ("going at least 50 miles an hour faster than the narrow street warranted") and respond with him. Readers perceive this scene through the filter of Bruce's consciousness.

Both writers generate tension, involve several senses, and contrast long sentences with short. Yet despite similarities, readers detect four distinct voices: one for each of the characters and another for each of the writers. A third passage, this one self-contained, presents two more voices.

"North Woods" — by Jan Schubert

She didn't realize she was being hunted. Not at the time. Not until later, after she'd left the woods to walk along the shoreline for a distance. She took her shoes off and waded to her ankles in the icy water of the big lake, letting the little waves slap up against her legs and the stiff breeze off the water cool her down before she re-entered the woods for her walk back to the cabin.

It was when she entered the woods again she first heard him. The air was humid and still away from the shore. Rain from the early morning had been changed to steam by the hot sun pressing down relentlessly on the thick trees and underbrush of the wild North Woods. She wasn't sure it was human at first, this little cough, like a wheezing animal, and then a faint shuddering in the trees a few yards off the path. It startled her a little, but not greatly. She just kept walking. The cabin wasn't far. But when she later found the car keys missing even though she was sure she had left them in the ignition, then she knew.

In two long paragraphs rather than several short ones, readers move even more directly inside the protagonist's head ("she didn't realize she was being hunted"). Again danger threatens, yet the imagery concentrates on the character's activities ("took her shoes off and waded," then "re-entered the woods") as well as the environment ("stiff breeze," "changed to steam," and "hot sun"). Schubert emphasizes the character's imminent peril only in the first and final sentences.

Technically, this scene is less immediate than the preceding two ("not at the time" and "not until later"). Yet tension develops through details that provide figurative as well as literal meaning. The ominous tone never evaporates from the physical description. The water is "icy," and "the little waves" don't caress or surround. They "slap." The trees are "thick" and the underbrush "wild." The environment becomes an enemy more dangerous than the sun "pressing down relentlessly." The character reacts only "a little," yet readers can't ignore the "faint shuddering of a wheezing animal." Dramatic irony, or readers realizing what a character doesn't, inspires further tension. Initially, this character doesn't recognize her predicament. Readers, however, have been worrying since the first sentence.

Analyzing perspective, syntax, pace, and imagery in these passages reveals how authors achieve particular effects and why their voices sound distinct. Yet none of this can capture the essence of voice. The total effect involves far more than the individual components, just as the sound of a chorus transcends the contribution of the altos, sopranos, and other participants.

HARMONIZING VOICES

The combined effect of character voices contributes to the fiction writer's voice. Whatever the point of view, when the narrator quits narrating, each character must sound unique. To illustrate, a conversation between Adam and Eve in the Garden of Eden could develop like this:

"Please, Eve," Adam begs her. "We are well aware of our responsibilities within this Garden we have been given."

She says nothing, only closes her eyes to picture the tastes, nibblings, pleasures.

Adam's speech and Eve's thoughts suggest two distinct voices. What would readers hear if Adam, Eve, and the serpent each narrated the Garden of Eden scenario?

Adam: We are well aware of our responsibilities within this garden we have been given. We will obey orders. Neither questions nor special circumstances justify deviation. Law is law. Rules are rules.

Eve: Opportunities, exquisitely innovative potentials perambulate here in Paradise. Picture the tastes, nibblings, pleasures. Imagine the tempting, proliferating contingencies. Such pleasurable possibilities—all perfect and all permanent.

Serpent: They'll be sorry. How come the dirty work's mine? I can pull this off. Orders, orders. Punishment, punishment. Says who? Can't push me around. Not me. No way. This is gonna be my party.

The above illustrates one of many possible interpretations. Three characters contrast in viewpoint, motivation, and goals. Each monologue resonates at a different pitch, so each character sounds like an individual. A singular sound should represent each singular personality.

FINDING YOUR VOICE

You yourself have a unique, genuine sound. Everyone does. Your true voice is creative, inventive, perhaps inspiring. As James Dickey reassures:

> After you've been writing—and failing—for a good long time then you develop a kind of critical sense about what you write. You can tell when something is good, but it would be just as good in somebody else's work, too. You want to hold out for those things only you can say; and two, that you judge it good even though it's something only you could say. These are rare times when you get something like that, but you can tell. You know it when you think to yourself, "Did I say that?" And then the other part of your brain answers, "Yes, I did." (Bruce Joel Hillman in Strickland, 183)

What a feeling! You relax; you grin; you sound irresistible. Words sail forth without fiddling with the tiller. You stay on course, gliding forward at more than your customary number of pages per hour. This is writing at its happiest: effortless, powerful, thrilling.

So what prevents this happening all the time? The struggle to convey meaning, emphasize a particular message, or even shift from one scene to another can obstruct your authentic voice. If you pour out your first draft from your uncensored self, you'll possess what you thought you wanted to say. Obviously, this option vanishes if you suppress your ideas from the start or hit *delete* the instant you type something. You can always edit what you write, but not until you've written it.

May Sarton suggests: "Never think of the effect of what you are doing while you are doing it. Don't project to a possible audience while you are writing. Hold on to your idea and get it down, and then maybe there'll be an audience." (Lois Rosenthal in Strickland, 158) Fantasies about acclaim and audience encourage artificial delivery, which your audience detects. Acclaimed writers often focus not on audience but word and idea. Write for yourself and what you want to express.

That pushes you past the negative packaging that everyone collects while moving through life. Like all adults, writers have experienced disappointment, embarrassment, loss, fear of failure, and drive to succeed. Moving toward your own voice involves shedding some of what you've learned and planned. You won't find your voice while trying to sound erudite, urbane, charming, or wry. Your voice won't emerge while you attempt to reproduce Ursula LeGuin or Stephen King, or while imagining a bestseller, blockbuster, or Great American Novel. Dreaming is wonderful. Fantasies about fame and fortune, though, can drown out your authentic voice.

Vulnerability

Somewhere deep inside, where expectations, censorship, insecurity, and competition disappear, your own voice thrives. You can recollect that artless voice at least dimly, because as a child you probably communicated with this voice alone. It survives and strengthens every time you generate thoughts, characters, and plots. So whenever you write anything at all (even a to-do list), listen for that voice. Listen even if the prospect of hearing the sound that's yours alone feels slightly scary.

Good writing often springs from areas you can't explore without vulnerability, although candor about self and others carries a price. Erica Jong believes that "Everyone has talent. What is rare is the courage to follow that talent to the dark place where it leads." (Shaughnessy, 5) Some writers must choose between safe security and the openness that the real (and thus most original) self offers. Can you confront difficult truths?

Some of those involve assessing the quality of your words. Do they please you because you judge them as a writer or as a reader? Do those words offer something, or are they merely material you worked on for weeks? Evaluating your fictional world and its wording resembles asking Susie's mom if little Susie is cute and talented or just average.

Honesty

Yet admit it or not, you already know when an opening seems dreary, a sentence awkward, or a transition so remote that readers plunge into a deep chasm between one scene and the next. Even when pages flood forth in your authentic voice, you must still return to polish and revise with a critical eye. Perhaps Susie's mom can't help herself. But you need ruthless honesty about identifying and repairing weak spots. Don't rationalize nagging doubts like "At least it's not as long as Faulkner's sentences," or "In conversation people bore each other all the time." Instead of silencing your protests, listen.

Listen to your sentences, and listen for your voice. The task is less manufacturing something than reclaiming what you already possess and either mislaid or buried. Let your characters speak. If at least one takes on the dimensions of a real human being, that voice can lead you to your own. According to Toni Morrison, "Whenever I feel uneasy about my writing, I think: What would be the response of the people in the book if they read the book? That's my way of staying on track. Those are the people for whom I write." (Winokur, 278) Bringing your characters to life can bring your voice to life.

Ego

If your characters become themselves, you're less likely to notice what impression you make and more likely to claim your voice. Picture a shy or self-conscious person at a party. Among large groups of people, unfamiliar ones in particular, Steve worries about being short, growing bald, making conversation, and looking like a fool. If Steve focuses on others, he stops worrying about himself. He could compliment Shelly's new hairdo or ask about Gary's surgery. Steve can wonder whether Hal's having a good time instead of whether Steve is.

As partygoer or writer, be other-directed. This is easier said than done, because it involves relinquishing ego. But by minimizing self-consciousness through thinking first about your characters and next about your readers, you downplay self. The less you think about you, the greater your chance of being you. Begin with character and end there. Dine and wine your characters to learn everything you can about who they are. The more you immerse yourself in your characters and their world, the better your chance of relating their story as no one else can.

But no matter how well you know your characters, you cannot shame or command your voice out of hiding. The flamboyant colors of autumn leaves that delight us each year don't appear magically. Instead, the chlorophyll disappears, so nothing disguises the brilliance that always existed underneath. Voice isn't a matter of splashing dazzling color onto the surface but revealing your true colors. After all the attention paid so far to *should*, remember that you find your voice by being yourself, by believing in yourself and your characters. That can empower you and provide the courage to let go.

Henry pecks Georgina's cheek. "Took my last final yesterday, and we're heading out. Just came to say goodbye."

For one of the few times in her life, Georgina has no words.

Ashley hugs the silent Georgina. "We brought you take-out...to say thanks."

"Errr, no need to thank me." Georgina looks inscrutable as a cat. "What will I...with you gone, there isn't any more to...Oh well, at least you finished the semester. Henry, are you sure that..."

"Georgina, you know I adore you, respect you and so on, but...you can't stop us!"

Checklist: Being Yourself

✓ Does your writing interest you?
✓ Are you trying to imitate anyone?
✓ Does your voice sound like you?
✓ Do your characters start taking themselves to dinner?
✓ Can readers distinguish your writing from everyone else's?

NO MORE STRETCHING EXERCISES FOR NOW

Maybe you've confined your writing to experimenting with these exercises. If so, you're probably ready for more. Does this prospect excite or intimidate you? One author confesses that

> I write for a couple of hours every day, even if I only get a couple of sentences. I put in that time. You do that every day, and inspiration will come along. I don't allow myself not to keep trying. It's not fun, but if you wait until you want to write, you'll never do it. (Shaughnessy, 98)

The humorous (and prolific!) syndicated columnist Dave Barry confesses this.

Many productive writers share your reluctance about beginning and continuing. Professional writers, though, lack the luxury of postponing what sometimes feels uncomfortable, discouraging, or just plain hard. Scheduling can assist even those who don't earn their living writing. If you produce fewer pages than you'd like, maybe reading or television is more habitual than writing. A journal can help. Wish you'd started earlier? It's still not too late. Quit worrying whether you admire a potential plot or trust that you'll ever type *The End*. Get something on paper. Chat with your characters. If you feed them extravagantly and coax their confessions, they'll be there to help. Complete a draft; revise it later.

This final checklist synthesizes preceding suggestions. If you revise enough, your draft can become the fiction you always wanted to write, read, and find on your bookshelf.

Checklist: Revision

✓ Is the title effective?
✓ Is the exposition integrated?
✓ Is your fictional world credible and consistent?
✓ Is the point of view apt and consistent?
✓ Do your characters become individuals with individual voices?
✓ Do you reveal character motivation?
✓ Do you balance narrative, dialogue, and scene?
✓ Does the conflict generate tension?
✓ Does the reader experience immediacy?
✓ Do you startle readers on the levels of character, plot, and language?
✓ Do you evoke several of the five senses?
✓ Are your transitions seamless?
✓ Have you included all the details needed—but nothing more?
✓ Does the wording blend into your fictional world?
✓ Do you waste no words?
✓ Do you understate?
✓ Is your style genuine?

LOOKING BACK, THEN AHEAD

Since Henry no longer picks the place for coffee, Georgina chooses The Den. It's close, and she's tired. She orders a fancy latte to cheer herself up. It's less thrilling than Henry proclaimed. She looks down at her empty pad, yawns, and checks out the room.

At the next table a tall guy studies a thin volume. She lets herself stare a little. Needs a haircut. Nice chin cleft. Most important, nicely enraptured by his reading. It's...it's...Emily Dickinson! What kind of guy reads Emily Dickinson! She checks for a wedding ring. Of course its absence proves nothing. Still, she'd have lots in common with a guy so immersed in Dickinson. Does he like spending time alone? This is great coffee. She'll jog her usual mile after all. Sipping her latte, she leans over the yellow pad. Does he read Dickinson at work? Does he like his job? Would he like to go out to dinner?

Georgina probably won't be alone long. Who knows what's ahead? A snack or two here, a meal or two there, and she'll soon be arguing about where to have coffee. She'll resume cajoling, domineering, and when necessary, compromising. She'll bring just one thing with her from that world to this new one: her own voice. How far will that take her?

CONCLUSION

The Writer's Reality

Planning to write is not writing. Outlining...researching...talking to people about what you're doing, none of that is writing. Writing is writing. (E.L. Doctorow in Jacobs, 51)

Brainstorming her new plot, Georgina gobbles popcorn. A familiar voice interrupts. "Dining again?"

"Henry! How are you?"

"We're great—I just didn't want to lose touch."

"Ah, Henry, I'll miss you."

"Me too. Couldn't we work together? I mean not right now—some time?"

"Lovely idea, but later. You know how much I love you, Henry, but there's this other...besides, you have your own life now."

There are no endings here, only recurrent beginnings. Writers don't always see it that way. One instructor expresses concern:

Young writers tend to think that the world will come to an end, and a happy one, when their first book appears; in fact all that means is that you now have your second one to write. It's not as if this is a game of tic-tac-toe, and once you figure out how to play it you can always get it right. It's a process, isn't it, as least as much as a result. (Delbanco in Neubauer, 71)

If you obsess over achieving what resembles the ultimate goal, it can elude you forever—just like finding your voice. Many writers want publication more than anything. Is that the only goal? Again, let go.

To gain the book, one must give up all hope for the book. It is the only way the book can get written. When one writes one cannot simultaneously be gazing up at a glorious, abstract painting of what the book should be, a painting that is all golden glow and admirable wordless heft conveying a sense of a book like a bible, like your very own bible—penned by you—and at the same time expect to be advancing into the body of this particular earthly book. It won't work. (Friedman, 111)

Yet many talented, would-be writers need external validation to continue.

Such validation feels wonderful. Few thrills rival seeing your work in print. Yet writers need perspective about that thrill or even its possibility. After all, "A phone doesn't ring and make you someone else." (Friedman, 144) Maybe someday someone will call about publishing your work. Maybe no one will. Neither instance correlates with your worth as a person or even a writer. Everyone knows that wonderful writing remains sequestered, while rubbish gets published.

Confidence and quality matter at least as much as publication. An objective eye helps you revise enough to believe in your work and produce writing pleasing to others. People who are neither editors nor publishers help develop that eye. Writers rely on fellow authors— always have. Consider relationships like George Sand and Gustave Flaubert, Edith Wharton and Henry James, or Virginia Woolf and Vita Sackville-West. Or investigate workshops, retreats, and university programs. These provide knowledge, advice, and support. If several editors say no thanks, it helps to have folks you respect insist that those editors don't know what they're missing.

Maybe, though, you crave validation from someone who isn't your mother, someone that doesn't like or even know you. Perhaps the pages don't come without someone shining the green light indicating keep going; you're a real writer. Ultimately, only you keep yourself writing. Are you spending your time wondering if you're good instead of writing? Get the words down. Then, to keep writing, consider Ernest Hemingway's suggestion:

> Stop when you are going good. If you do that you'll never be stuck. And don't think or worry about it until you start to write again the next day. That way your subconscious will be working on it all the time, but if you worry about it, your brain will get tired before you start again. But work every day. No matter what has happened the day or night before, get up and bite on the nail. (Edward P. Stafford in Strickland, 25)

Not all writers can manage this. Georgina would never quit when her writing glides as if propelled by wind alone. Many writers complete their best work consciously struggling with the next page, miles from writing desk or computer. But part of Hemingway's message applies to us all: the more you "bite on the nail" when you feel you haven't the heart for it, the easier biting becomes. Habitual writers are open to the words and ideas hunting for writers.

Trust yourself, your characters, and your voice. Become familiar with your characters and your voice at the deepest levels of your being. Then enjoy your characters and your voice: that's the primary goal of this book.

Wherever you go next, I hope you will be writing there.

GLOSSARY

Note: These terms often have a specific meaning when related to fiction. All the definitions below reflect that specific meaning.

Abstract: Language lacking concreteness or specificity, e.g., concepts like love, patriotism, war, significance.

Allusion: An explicit or indirect reference to mythology, religion, history, a different work of literature or art, or other common reference, such as a television program or a sport.

Ambiguity: Wording that purposefully allows for more than one meaning, perhaps on both literal and symbolic levels, e.g., she watched in horror as the stain spread over her wedding dress.

Antagonist: The main opponent or foil, someone who obstructs the progress of the primary character.

Anachronism: Deliberate or accidental incongruity pertaining to time frame, such as the modern newspaper Merlyn receives in the Camelot of T. H. White's *The Once and Future King.*

Archetype: Original or idealized image from folklore or mythology that conveys human commonality and suggests characters and situations of great depth.

Aside: In theatre, a convention that a character can share musings with audience or self. Fiction treats this device as a monologue.

Backstory: Contextual material, also referred to as exposition, that precedes the relevant conflict.

Catharsis: According to Aristotle, the emotional cleansing resulting from the pity and fear experienced from viewing the downfall of a tragic hero.

Cavalry Save: A non-believable resolution of a problem, e.g. the cavalry neatly and improbably enters to save a damsel in distress. Aristotle had labeled this *deus ex machina.*

Cliché: An overworked, familiar expression that no longer produces a vivid image, e.g., she is as dead as a doornail.

Climax: The most exciting or dramatic moment, or the point when the conclusion becomes inevitable.

Coherence: A sense of unity arising from characterization, plot, point of view, setting, and style contributing to a unified whole.

Comic relief: Release from tension following intense drama or tragedy.

Complications: One or more difficulties, sometimes called the rising action, that block character progress toward some goal or resolution.

Compression: Elimination of unnecessary words.

Concrete: Details that can be experienced through one or more of the five senses: sight, sound, taste, smell, or touch, e.g., sunrise, thunder, apples, lavender, fur.

Conflict: The source of tension generated by opposition between the characters and external forces or conditions, i.e., character versus self, someone, or something.

Connotation: The implied meaning that suggests something beyond the literal meaning or denotation, e.g., *blood* red (a color that creates a negative atmosphere by conjuring wounds, danger, or death).

Deconstruction: A renovated version of something familiar created by reassembling the original components in a new and thus startling way, e.g., the tale of Cinderella narrated from the viewpoint of her stepmother.

Delay: Material that slows down the unraveling of the storyline.

Denotation: The literal or exact dictionary meaning of a word or phrase, e.g., red (a pigment referring to a particular part of the color spectrum).

Denouement: The falling action or ordering of loose ends or complications following the climax.

Deus ex Machina: A non-believable resolution of a problem devised by an otherworldly contrivance that miraculously sets things right—now often called the "cavalry save."

Dialect: A particular speech pattern associated with a specific geographical area, ethnic group, or subculture. Often a few alterations of word choice, order, or spelling can suggest this.

Diction: Word choice.

Dramatic Irony: A conflict in expectations that arises from readers having information about the situation that is unavailable to one or more of the characters, e.g., long before Oedipus Rex, the audience knows that he will murder his father and marry his mother.

Duplicity: An image that simultaneously functions on both literal and figurative levels, e.g., a squirrel climbing on the birdfeeder represents part of the setting as well as the attributes of determination and adroitness.

Epiphany: A sudden realization of a significant truth, often brought on by grappling with the conflict, e.g., a grief-stricken Oedipus Rex eventually realizes that he has murdered his father and married his mother.

Explosion: A dramatic moment, event, or difficulty that immediately intrigues readers.

Exposition: Background material, also referred to as backstory, which readers require in order to understand the context of the characters and plot.

Falling Action: The slacking off following the climax or turning point.

Fictional World: The *more real than reality* realm that readers inhabit while immersed in a short story or novel.

Figurative Language: Non-literal comparisons used for description, including metaphor and simile, e.g., pure as a mountain spring or velvet fur.

First Person Point of View: Narration presented from the perspective of an *I* narrator who is present even if not directly involved in events, e.g., I watched the truck approach at top speed.

Flashback: A return to events that occurred prior to the storyline.

Flesh out: To give a character or scene substance in order to create the illusion of a multi-dimensional fictional world.

Foil: A character that contrasts with another character in order to highlight a trait like greed or a goal like financial security.

Foreshadowing: A hint or series of clues suggesting or foretelling what will occur later.

Genre: A specialized category such as science fiction, mystery, romance, western, or magical realism.

Hubris: A classical term for the sin of pride, usually resulting in the downfall of a tragic hero such as Oedipus Rex or Macbeth.

Illusion of Reality: The suggestion that a fictional world seems more convincing and intriguing than a literal recapturing of actual people or events.

Imagery: Concrete description that is either literal or figurative, e.g., a lake glittering in the sunlight, or the sunlight scatters a trail of diamonds on the lake.

Irony: The contrast between what is expected and what occurs.

Limited Point of View: A perspective where the author narrates in third person but filters events through the perceptions of one character.

Literal: A true-to-life, realistic description involving no symbolic or figurative meaning.

Melodrama: A work generating intense emotion by presenting oversimplified and stereotypical rather than realistic characters and situations, such as a villain threatening a heroine.

Metafiction: A short story or novel that interrupts reader immersion in the narrative by calling attention to the characters, the author's voice, and/or the nature of fiction.

Metaphor: A direct, non-literal comparison, e.g., a rose is love.

Mixed Metaphor: A figurative comparison that confuses readers with unclear, inconsistent, or unlikely relationships, e.g., love grew in me like a building that flung me into a volcano of confusion.

Monologue: A passage of introspection or conversation with self, which is comparable to the aside in theater.

Motif: A literal or figurative concept, image, or phrase that is deliberately repeated in order to achieve an effect.

Mouthpiece: A character who conveys the beliefs or viewpoint of the author.

Objective Correlative: The poet T.S. Eliot's term for a concrete image of the external world, such as a scene or a group of items suggesting an internal landscape, e.g., a graveyard or a stormy night.

Objective Point of View: The plot events expressed from the perspective of a narrator who only reports, functioning like a camera.

Omniscient Point of View: The third person perspective where the author knows everything and can see inside all the characters.

Pacing: The rate at which writers relate the events or conversation of a narrative.

Pathetic Fallacy: A literary convention that compares some aspect of nature with a character so that the external world represents internal emotions, e.g., the protagonist weeps, and the skies drizzle.

Plot: The events of the narrative.

Plot Structure: The ordering of the events included in the narrative, from conflict to climax, possibly followed by falling action and resolution.

Point of View: The perspective (first, second, or third person) used to convey the events of the plot.

Protagonist: The main or central character.

Resolution: The solution to the conflict or difficulty within a character, community, or environment.

Resonance: The creation of characters, images, and events that suggest overtones reminiscent of readers' own experiences, thus enabling them to identify with the fictional world.

Retrospective Point of View: A first person perspective expressed by a narrator after events have already occurred, usually creating tension between innocence and experience.

Scene: A visceral enactment of characters in conflict, creating movement rather than inactivity, and suggesting the illusion of a motion picture rather than a photograph or a summary.

Scenario: A detailed outline of the events that the plot includes.

Second Person Point of View: Narration presented from the perspective of a *you* narrator, as if the reader participates in events e.g., you watched the truck approach at top speed.

Setting: The time, location, context, and atmosphere where the plot takes place.

Simile: A non-literal comparison that calls attention to the corresponding relationship by using words such as *like, as*, or *resembles*, e.g., love is like a rose.

Stereotype: A stock character or predictable situation that lacks originality.

Storyline: The plot events involving the decisions or actions of the main character from the beginning to the end, starting at or just before the conflict and usually including complications, climax, falling action, and resolution.

Style: The way a writer communicates the material, i.e., word choice, sentence structure, tone, imagery, and plot structure.

Subtext: The unwritten meaning that readers infer from what is implied rather than expressed through the dialogue or description.

Subjective Point of View: The plot events viewed through the filter of one character, conveyed from a first person, second person, third person limited, or omniscient perspective.

Suspension of Disbelief: The unwritten contract between writer and reader to disregard the customary boundaries of reality while visiting the fictional world.

Symbol: An image or object that stands for something else, e.g., a bluebird represents happiness.

Syntax: Sentence structure.

Tension: The balance between opposing forces that keeps readers wondering about the final outcome of the plot.

Texture: The features that add layers of richness and resonance to characterization, plot, setting, and imagery.

Theme: The main idea, point, moral stance, or primary emphasis of a short story or novel.

Third Person Point of View: Narration presented from the perspective of a *he, she, or it* narrator, e.g., she watched the truck approach at top speed.

Tone: The expression of the author's attitude toward the subject, e.g., humorous, ironic, or satirical.

Transition: Image, symbol, dialogue, or other device used to join each scene, paragraph, or description with what follows.

Understatement: Use of a restrained tone, particularly when dealing with a tragic situation or theme.

Unreliable Narrator: The device of relating events from the perspective of a character who is deceitful, delusional, or unaware of all the implications of the situation.

Universal: The perception that the material applies to everyone rather than to a particular individual or group.

Verisimilitude: The impression that a fictional world is more credible than actual events or people.

Viewpoint: Attitude or belief system.

Voice: The combination of tone, style, and phrasing that projects an author's singular personality onto the page. This captures the sensation that one sounds exactly like oneself without being artificial or manipulative.

BIBLIOGRAPHY

Austen, Jane. *Mansfield Park*, ed. R.W. Chapman, 3rd ed. London: Oxford University Press, 1934.

Camp, Wesley D. *What a Piece of Work Is Man*. Englewood Cliffs, New Jersey, Prentice Hall, 1990.

Charlton, James, ed. *The Writer's Quotation Book*. New York: Penguin, 1981.

Cook, Marshall J. *The Year of the Buffalo*. Superior: Savage Press, 1997.

DeSmet, Christine. *Spirit Lake*. Hard Shell Word Factory: www.hardshell.com, 2000.

Eliot, T.S. *The Sacred Wood*. New York: Barnes & Noble, 1960.

Evans, Bergen. *Dictionary of Quotations*. New York: Bonanza, 1958.

Friedman, Bonnie. *Writing Past Dark: Envy, Fear, Distraction, and Other Dilemmas in the Writer's Life*. New York: Harper Perennial. 1993.

Gardner, John. *The Art of Fiction: Notes on Craft for Young Writers*. New York: Vintage, 1983.

Gerard, Philip. *Creative Nonfiction: Researching and Crafting Stories of Real Life*. Ohio: Story Press, 1996.

Horgan, Paul. *Approches to Writing*. New York: Farrar, Straus, and Giroux, 1968.

Jacobs, Ben and Helena Hjalmarsson. *The Quotable Book Lover*. New York: Lyons Press, 1999.

Lodge, David. *The Art of Fiction*. New York: Viking, 1992.

Neubauer, Alexander. *Conversations on Writing Fiction: Interviews with Thirteen Distinguished Teachers of Fiction Writing in America*. New York: Harper Perennial, 1994.

Rich, Adrienne. *What Is Found There: Notebooks on Poetry and Politics*. New York: Quality Paperbacks, 1993.

Shaughnessy, Susan. *Walking on Alligators: A Book of Meditations for Writers*. San Francisco: Harper, 1993.

Stein, Sol. *Stein on Writing*. New York: St. Martin's Press, 1995.

Stephens, Meic. *Collins Dictionary of Literary Quotations*. Glasgow: Harper Collins, 1990.

Strickland, Bill, ed. *On Being a Writer.* Cincinnati: Writer's Digest Books, 1989.

Trimble, John R. *Writing with Style.* Englewood Cliffs, New Jersey: Prentice-Hall, 1975.

Wasson, John M. *Subject and Structure.* Boston: Little, Brown, and Company, 1972.

Watt, William W. *An American Rhetoric.* New York: Holt, Rinehart, and Winston, 1980, 5th edition.

Winokur, Jon. *Writers on Writing.* Philadelphia: Running Press, 1990.

Woodworth, Deborah. *A Deadly Shaker Spring.* New York: Avon, 1998.

ADDITIONAL SOURCES

Literature

Allison, Dorothy. *Bastard out of Carolina.* New York: Plume, 1992.

Barrie, James. *Peter Pan and Other Plays.* London: Oxford Drama Library, 1995.

Beckett, Samuel. *Waiting for Godot.* New York: Grove Press, 1954.

Brönte, Emily. *Wuthering Heights.* New York: The Modern Library, 1950.

Brown, Rosellen. *Before and After.* New York: Farrar Straus Giroux, 1992.

Brown, Wesley and Amy Ling, eds. *Imagining America: Stories from the Promised Land.* New York: Persea Books, 1991.

Carver, Raymond. *Cathedral.* New York: Vintage Contemporaries, 1984.

Conrad, Josef. *Heart of Darkeness & The Secret Sharer.* New York: Signet Classics, 1950.

Dickens, Charles. *Great Expectations.* New York: Holt, Rinehart, and Winston, 1963.

Dorris, Michael. *A Yellow Raft in Blue Water.* New York: Warner Books, 1987.

Fitzgerald, F. Scott. *The Great Gatsby.* New York: Charles Scribner's Sons, 1953.

Forster, E.M. *A Passage to India.* New York: Harcourt Brace Jovanovich, 1952.

Godwin, Gail. *Father Melancholy's Daughter.* New York: William Morrow and Co., Inc., 1991.

Guterson, David. *Snow Falling on Cedars.* New York: Vintage Contemporaries, 1995.

Hardy, Thomas. *The Return of the Native.* New York: Holt, Rinehart, and Winston, 1963.

Hawthorne, Nathaniel. *The Scarlet Letter.* New York: Bantam, 1981.

Hemingway, Ernest. *The Old Man and the Sea.* New York: Charles Scribner's Sons, 1952.

Hemingway, Ernest. *In Our Time.* New York: Charles Scribner's Sons, 1958.

Joyce, James. *Dubliners,* Robert Scholes and A. Walton Litz, eds. New York: The Viking Press, 1969.

Keneally, Thomas. *Schindler's List.* New York: A Touchstone Book, 1993.

Kesey, Ken. *Sometimes a Great Notion.* New York: A Bantam Book, 1969.

Kiernan, Kathy and Michael M. Moore, eds. *First Fiction.* Boston: Little, Brown, and Co., 1994.

Kingston, Maxine Hong. *China Men.* New York: Vintage International, 1980.

Lee, Chang-Rae. *Native Speaker.* New York: Riverhead, 1995.

Lee, Harper.*To Kill a Mockingbird.* New York: Harper Collins, 1995.

LeGuin, Ursula. *The Left Hand of Darkness.* New York: Harper & Row, 1969.

Litz, A. Walton. *Major American Short Stories.* New York: Oxford University Press, 1980.

McCourt, Frank. *Angela's Ashes.* New York: Scribner, 1996.

Melville, Herman. *Moby Dick,* Harrison Hayford and Hershel Parker, eds. New York: W.W. Norton & Company, 1967.

Miller, Arthur. *Death of a Salesman.* New York: Dramatists Play Service, 1998.

Mizener, Arthur, ed. *Modern Short Stories: The Uses of Imagination,* 4th ed. New York: W.W. Norton, 1979.

Moskowitz, Faye, ed. *Her Face in the Mirror: Jewish Women on Mothers and Daughters.* Boston: Beacon Press, 1994.

Orwell, George. *Animal Farm.* New York: Harcourt, Brace and Company, 1946.

Pickering, James H., ed. *Fiction 100: An anthology of Short Stories*, 7th edition. Englewood Cliffs: Prentice Hall, 1995.

Proust, Marcel. *Swann's Way*. Penguin Great Books of the 20th Century, 1999.

Rölvaag, O.E. *The Boat of Longing*. St. Paul: Minnesota Historical Society Press, 1985.

Rowling, J.K. *Harry Potter and the Sorcerer's Stone*. New York: Arthur A. Levine, 1999.

Shakespeare, William. *Hamlet*, Alfred Harbage, ed. New York: Viking, 1977.

Shakespeare, William. *King Lear*, Alfred Harbage, ed. New York: Viking, 1977.

Shakespeare, William. *Macbeth*, Alfred Harbage, ed. New York: Viking, 1977.

Shelley, Mary. *Frankenstein*. New York: Bantam Pathfinder Editions, 1973.

Sophocles, *Oedipus Rex*. Dover Thrift, 1993.

Stegner, Wallace. *Angle of Repose*. New York: Penguin Books, 1971.

Steinbeck, John. *The Grapes of Wrath*. New York: Bantam, 1972.

Tan, Amy. *The Joy Luck Club*. New York: Ivy, 1989.

Tan, Amy. *The Hundred Secret Senses*. New York: Ivy, 1995.

Twain, Mark. *Huckleberry Finn*. New York: Harper and Brothers, 1912.

White, T.H. *The Once and Future King*. New York: Berkley Medallion, 1940.

Woolf, Virginia. *To the Lighthouse*. New York: Harcourt, Brace & Company, 1927.

Texts on Writing

Camenson, Blythe and Marshall J. Cook. *Your Novel Proposal: from Creation to Contract*. Cincinnati: Writer's Digest Books, 1999.

Els, Susan McBride. *Into the Deep: A Writer's Look at Creativity*. Portsmouth: Heinemann, 1994.

Guthrie, A.B. *A Field Guide to Writing Fiction*. New York: Harper Collins, 1991.

Moyers, Bill. *A World of Ideas*. New York: Doubleday, 1989.

Seger, Linda. *Creating Unforgettable Characters: a Practical Guide to Character Development in Films, TV Series, Advertisements, Novels & Short Stories*. New York: Owl, 1990.

Stern, Jerome. *Making Shapely Fiction.* New York: Laurel, 1991.

Tobias, Ronald B. *20 Master Plots (and How to Build Them).* Cincinnati: Writer's Digest Books, 1993.

Woodson, Linda. *The Writer's World.* New York: Harcourt Brace Jovanovich, 1986.

INDEX

ABOUT THE AUTHOR

Dr. Laurel Yourke, of the University of Wisconsin—Madison Department of Liberal Studies and the Arts, has received two prestigious teaching awards. In 1997 the Chancellor of the University of Wisconsin honored her with a campus-wide Award for Excellence in Teaching. She was recognized again in 1999, when the Council of Wisconsin Writers selected her for the Christopher Robert Scholes Award for Encouragement of Wisconsin Writers.

For three decades Dr. Yourke has been reaching writing students aged eight to eighty. She has presented creative writing through such avenues as interactive television, University Outreach, Elderhostel, Chautauqua, School of the Arts, Write by the Lake, and Writer's Institute. She has also taught on campus and created several Distance Education courses.

Yourke has published her own poetry in various university and small presses and served as Series Consultant for the award-winning series, *The Courage to Write*.

Take Your Characters to Dinner is the result of over thirty years writing and teaching experience and synthesizes the insights gained during a diverse teaching career.